Taking Control of Anxiety is essential ̶ ̶ ̶ ̶ ̶ ̶ ̶ ̶ ̶ ̶ ̶ ̶ ̶ ̶ ̶ .nx-iety disorders and for those who treat such individuals. It is filled with practical, evidence-based suggestions on ways to reduce anxiety and enhance well-being. Moore, who is one of the leaders in the field, deserves kudos for including work-sheets, exercises, inspiring quotable quotes, and appropriate cautionary notes.

—**Don Meichenbaum, PhD,** author of *Roadmap to Resilience: A Guide for Military, Trauma Victims and Their Families;* Research Director of the Melissa Institute for Violence Prevention, Miami, FL

Moore has done a superb job explaining how to become proactive in managing your anxiety. He speaks in the voice of a storyteller and teacher with an easy-to-read, authoritative, and reassuring style. Part mentor, part fact giver, and even part cheerleader, Moore provides empowering information and action-oriented tips on how to participate in your own recovery from anxiety or how to help a loved one.

—**Stephen M. Stahl MD, PhD,** Professor of Psychiatry, University of California, San Diego; Honorary Visiting Senior Fellow, University of Cambridge, UK; Editor-in-Chief, *CNS Spectrums*

This book is a gem. It provides practical exercises in a very readable manner that helps anxious individuals manage their worry and get their life moving forward positively. Share this book with anyone you know who struggles with anxiety and worry.

—**Jeffrey E. Barnett, PsyD, ABPP,** Professor and Associate Chair, Department of Psychology, Loyola University, Maryland, Baltimore

Moore helps people with various anxiety-related problems understand why they are struggling, and he presents useful strategies for regaining a sense of control. His writing is very conversational and reassuring and the weekly experiments in anx-iety reduction are particularly engaging. All readers will find at least some of these suggestions to be very helpful as part of a consistent anxiety-reduction strategy. This book can be used on its own or as a workbook for clients in psychotherapy.

—**Richard Tedeschi, PhD,** Professor of Psychology, University of North Carolina, Charlotte

TAKING
CONTROL
OF
ANXIETY

TAKING CONTROL

OF

ANXIETY

SMALL STEPS FOR GETTING THE BEST OF WORRY, STRESS, AND FEAR

BRET A. MOORE

American Psychological Association • *Washington, DC*

Published by
APA LifeTools
American Psychological Association
750 First Street, NE
Washington, DC 20002
www.apa.org

To order
APA Order Department
P.O. Box 92984
Washington, DC 20090-2984
Tel: (800) 374-2721;
Direct: (202) 336-5510
Fax: (202) 336-5502;
TDD/TTY: (202) 336-6123
Online: www.apa.org/pubs/books
E-mail: order@apa.org

In the U.K., Europe, Africa, and the Middle East, copies may be ordered from
American Psychological Association
3 Henrietta Street
Covent Garden, London
WC2E 8LU England

Typeset in Sabon by Circle Graphics, Inc., Columbia, MD

Printer: Edwards Brothers, Inc., Ann Arbor, MI
Cover Designer: Naylor Design, Washington, DC

The opinions and statements published are the responsibility of the authors, and such opinions and statements do not necessarily represent the policies of the American Psychological Association.

Library of Congress Cataloging-in-Publication Data
Moore, Bret A.
  Taking control of anxiety : small steps for getting the best of worry, stress, and fear / Bret A. Moore, PsyD, ABPP. — First edition.
      pages cm
  Includes bibliographical references and index.
  ISBN-13: 978-1-4338-1747-2
  ISBN-10: 1-4338-1747-0
  1. Anxiety. 2. Anxiety—Treatment. 3. Self-help techniques. I. Title.

BF575.A6M65 2014
152.4'6—dc23
                            2014000558

British Library Cataloguing-in-Publication Data
A CIP record is available from the British Library.

Printed in the United States of America
First Edition

http://dx.doi.org/10.1037/14434-000

To Lori and Kaitlyn—for your laughter, love, understanding, and patience.

CONTENTS

Contents

ACKNOWLEDGMENTS

There are many people who make a book like this possible. I would like to thank Maureen Adams for helping me develop the original proposal. I have valued her help as an editor for many years. I am grateful for the dedicated and highly skilled staff at the American Psychological Association, including Daniel Brachtesende, Jennifer Meidinger, Nikki Seifert, Ron Teeter, and David Becker. I would especially like to thank Susan Herman for her helpful edits and suggestions on early versions of the manuscript. I am also indebted to the many experts who have shaped my thinking about anxiety, particularly its varied manifestations and most effective interventions. I have had the privilege to work with and learn from pioneers like Art Freeman, Don Meichenbaum, Stephen Stahl, and Art Jongsma. I am also grateful to those with whom I have not worked but whose writings have influenced my understanding of anxiety. The most notable are Edmund Bourne, David Barlow, Jon Kabat-Zinn, David Burns, Aaron Beck, and Judith Beck. The foundation of this book is based on the ideas, theories, and research of these individuals.

ANXIETY: AN INTRODUCTION

Anxiety is the dizziness of freedom

—Soren Kierkegaard

Late one Saturday night after a concert, Lori began to feel uneasy while walking to her car in the parking garage. She started thinking about her friend who was assaulted a few weeks back. She began to walk faster. Her heart began racing; she broke into a sweat. She felt like she couldn't catch her breath and her chest was tight. She just knew she was in trouble and that something bad was about to happen. After reaching her car, she jumped in and locked the doors. But she could not drive. Her hands were trembling and she felt dizzy. After 5 minutes or so, she felt better and was able to drive home. For several days afterward, all she could think about was how terrified she'd felt that night.

David was an A student and a highly acclaimed athlete in high school. Things always came easily for him. It wasn't until he failed a midterm exam during his second semester in college that he started doubting his abilities. He began worrying about future tests, wondering whether he would fail them as well. Although he didn't fail any other exams, his worry about the possibility of failing made it difficult for him to study. This caused his grades to drop from As to Bs and Cs. Things got worse. He began worrying about his future, particularly his career. If he was only an average student— or worse, flunked out of college—he'd never get a good job.

Without a good job, no woman would ever want to marry him. David believed he was destined for a life of disappointment and unhappiness.

Marie hit a rough patch in her life. Not only did she lose her job in a tough economy, her boyfriend of three years left her for another woman. If that wasn't enough, her elderly mother was hospitalized after falling and breaking her hip, which left her ailing father at home to care for himself. Marie's only sibling, an older brother, was of no help, as he had cut off all ties from his parents after leaving home. Consequently, the responsibility of caring for her parents fell squarely on her shoulders. Marie thought, "Why is it one thing after the other? My boyfriend left me, my parents are sick, and I don't know how I'm going to pay next month's rent. It's just too much for me to handle."[1]

If you are like most people, you can identify with the stories of Lori, David, and Marie to some degree. Perhaps you can identify with more than one of them. They are average people, who for varied reasons, are confronted with anxiety. Anxiety is as much of the current American culture as are reality television, online shopping, and cell phones. It is interwoven into our collective psyche so much that we spend billions of dollars each year trying to understand it, minimize its impact on our daily lives, or get rid of it completely. We worry about our careers. We stress about meeting next month's mortgage or rent. We obsess over the neatness of our homes. And we stay up late at night wondering whether we've forgotten something we should have done today or should do tomorrow. We can't help ourselves—it's just part of who we are. But the good news is

---

[1]All case examples in this book are fictional.

that anxiety doesn't have to control you. With a bit of knowledge, awareness, and a few simple techniques, you can effectively control your anxiety.

> Anxiety doesn't have to control you.

Notice that I said "control." Controlling your anxiety is a reasonable goal. Ridding yourself of anxiety is not. If your goal is to rid yourself of anxiety, you are setting yourself up for failure. Anxiety is part of the human experience. In fact, you wouldn't want to completely rid yourself of it if you could. Anxiety, in its various forms, is adaptive and serves critical functions, as I discuss below. The key is how you manage your anxiety through self-regulation, understanding, and acceptance. Trying to eliminate anxiety from your daily experience will leave you feeling frustrated and defeated.

WHAT IS ANXIETY?

Worry, stress, tension, nervousness, panic, fear, unease, jitters, angst, and the ever popular "heebie-jeebies" are all used to describe anxiety. However, these terms are not completely interchangeable. Although definitions vary in their complexity, anxiety is generally viewed as an unpleasant feeling of apprehension, concern, or dread. It's a palpable feeling of unease and unrest, and is often cryptic in its cause, difficult to describe, and a challenge to ignore.

There are three terms, however, that share similarities and are most often used to describe anxiety: worry, fear, and stress. *Worry* is what we do to ourselves by thinking too much. Worry in itself is not a big deal. It's unlikely a day goes by that you don't worry about something. But, as is clear in David's story, worry can become problematic if it starts to infiltrate many areas of your life. More important, if it causes you emotional, work/school, or relationship problems, it's time to do something about it. Again, worrying about bills or your child from time to time is generally of little concern. Worrying about many things all the time is more problematic.

Fear, the most primitive form of anxiety, is the emotional response to a known or suspected threat. It often shows itself through panic, as described in the vignette of Lori. Fear is considered to be a primitive emotion because it has served an important function in the evolution of humans. In fact, it continues to serve an important function in modern society, although for slightly different reasons. As discussed in later chapters, fear and panic are warning systems that help people make quick and important decisions about their safety and the safety of others. In some cases, in the absence of a real threat, people's warning systems malfunction, leaving them feeling embarrassed and emotionally and physically drained.

Stress, a term that is used to describe just about everything psychologically and physically unpleasant, is what the body and mind experience when life's demands are greater than what people feel they can handle or should be required to endure. If you don't believe me, over the next few days, listen to how many times you hear someone say they are *stressed* about work, school, parenthood, finances, health, marriage, friendships, traffic, chores, and so on. It has become a catchall term in today's culture. It's a hodgepodge of the various forms of anxiety, fatigue, exhaustion, emotional and physical pain, and a few other ingredients thrown in for good measure, but it remains in the anxiety family.

So, if I've lost you with my various descriptions and definitions of anxiety, don't worry. Throughout the book I use the term *anxiety* to describe worry, stress, fear, panic, and the like. The techniques I describe work for them all. However, if nuance is needed to understand a certain point, I let you know. The key point to remember is that anxiety is a complex emotional and physical phenomenon that takes different forms for different people. And, most important, you are not powerless against it.

THE GOOD AND THE BAD OF ANXIETY

At times, anxiety gets an undeserved bad rap. Just like alcohol, fast food, and slot machines, most everything is harmless in moderation— Anxiety is no different. Actually, some anxiety can be helpful. Not unlike Goldilocks's appreciation for perfectly warmed porridge, a "just right" amount of anxiety can bring about contentment. It also improves physical and mental performance, counters fatigue, and motivates people to do things they would otherwise avoid. Through its various physical manifestations, anxiety plays an important role in communication. It can let someone know that we feel uncomfortable, nervous, or even afraid. Without saying a word, it can communicate "I need some space" or "I'm not comfortable with what you are saying or doing." This may be particularly true (and helpful) for members of some cultural groups that are less comfortable vocalizing concerns or emotions to people outside their close social network. Anxiety can also communicate interest and attraction to another person. A man whose voice trembles every time he's around an attractive woman or a teenage girl who giggles, avoids eye contact, and blushes in the presence of a potential prom date are prime examples. The problem is that it's difficult to define what that right amount of anxiety is. The amount that's optimal for you may cause someone else to shut down. Regardless, anxiety is a good thing if you can find the right balance.

So, when is anxiety considered a problem? It depends. As I mentioned earlier, anxiety is a

Some anxiety can be helpful.

7

> If anxiety causes persistent and serious disruption in major areas of your life, then it is likely a problem.

part of our culture. If you don't experience at least a mild degree of anxiety, then you should probably be anxious about why you aren't experiencing any! However, a general rule of thumb is that if anxiety causes persistent and serious disruption in major areas of your life (family, work, social relationships), then it is likely a problem.

So, what is "serious disruption?" It depends on the person. We all react differently to different types and levels of stress and anxiety. For example, if a teacher is worried about whether her students will meet the school's performance standards next month and experiences a few nights of insomnia as a result, then this will likely be seen as more of a temporary nuisance. However, if this same teacher experiences continuous sleep problems, which leads to her being written up for coming in late to work, or if she experiences an increase in irritability, which leads to increased fighting between her and her husband, then this likely needs to be addressed. It doesn't mean that she is "pathological," "sick," or "crazy"; it could just mean that she needs a little extra help dealing with life's normal struggles. This help could include talking with a counselor, friend, family member, or religious/spiritual leader; going for a walk several times each week; or reading a self-help book such as this one.

HOW BIG IS THE PROBLEM?

Now that you know that day-to-day anxiety effects almost everyone, you may be wondering, how many of us go on to develop a full-blown psychiatric disorder? According to the National Institute of Mental Health, approximately 18% of American adults have experienced an anxiety disorder over the past year.[2] This translates to around 40 million people who are impacted to the point where professional intervention may be warranted. Out of those 40 million, only around 15 million actually seek treatment.[3]

> 18% of American adults have experienced an anxiety disorder over the past year.

This means that the vast majority of people manage their anxiety without the help of psychotherapy or medication. This can be good news or bad news, depending on how you look at it. The cynic would say that there are millions of highly distressed people walking around who need help. The optimist would likely argue that people are highly resilient and can manage even high levels of distress with their own personal resources. I tend to believe that it's more of the latter: Most of us, whether or not we know it, already use a variety of techniques to manage stress. This book will help you identify and refine those already existing techniques, as well as provide you with some additional ones.

HOW IS ANXIETY DIAGNOSED?

If you see a mental health professional for your anxiety, chances are you will be given a formal diagnosis, and maybe more than one.

---

[2]National Institute of Mental Health. (n.d.). *The numbers count: Mental disorders in America*. Retrieved from http://www.nimh.nih.gov/health/publications/the-numbers-count-mental-disorders-in-america/index.shtml#Anxiety

[3]Kessler, R. C., Chiu, W. T., Demler, O., & Walters, E. E. (2005). Prevalence, severity, and comorbidity of 12-month *DSM–IV* disorders in the National Comorbidity Survey Replication (NCS-R). *Archives of General Psychiatry, 62,* 617–27. doi:0.1001/archpsyc.62.6.617

The *Diagnostic and Statistical Manual of Mental Disorders—DSM* for short—is a publication by the American Psychiatric Association and is often referred to as the "psychiatric bible" (the latest version is the fifth edition: *DSM–5*).[4] The *DSM* houses several different anxiety-related disorders and provides diagnostic labels and codes for each. Mental health professionals rely on these psychiatric labels for several reasons. First, and probably foremost, it allows health care providers to get paid. Insurance companies generally do not reimburse for mental health services unless a formal diagnosis is submitted. Second, diagnostic labels allow mental health professionals to communicate with each other. For example, if a person is seen by one doctor and transfers to another, a diagnosis, in theory, provides the new doctor general information about the person's mental health status. And last, diagnoses help scientists conduct research on particular groups of people, or more appropriately, symptoms, which help determine which treatments are most effective for which disorders.

I mention the *DSM* because I believe it's important that a person be aware of the practice of diagnosing by mental health professionals. There is a deep and wide debate about the validity, reliability, motivations, and ethics associated with the *DSM*, particularly the *DSM–5*. Some critics of the practice feel that it pathologizes (labels people as sick when they aren't) normal reactions to stress and lumps people into narrow and poorly defined categories. Others believe the main purpose of the book is to promote psychiatry, a profession that relies primarily on the use of medications to

---

[4]American Psychiatric Association. (2013). *Diagnostic and statistical manual of mental disorders* (5th ed.). Arlington, VA: American Psychiatric Publishing.

treat psychiatric conditions.[5,6] Indeed, there is tremendous financial incentive for the profession and pharmaceutical companies to elevate pharmacology as the premier option for treating mental health issues. As with most things in life, however, the truth likely resides somewhere in the middle.[7]

With all that being said, the most important thing to keep in mind is that your symptoms may look similar to someone else's but the way you experience them is not the same as someone else might; therefore, you shouldn't be viewed the same or treated the same. You are the expert of *you*. And you know what works best for *you*. Don't let anyone try to convince you otherwise. See the List of Major Anxiety Disorders for your reference.

WHERE DOES ANXIETY COME FROM, AND WHY DOES IT STAY?

Trying to find a single cause for your anxiety will leave you frustrated and dissatisfied. This is, because anxiety is caused by many factors. There is no one gene, life experience, or neurochemical that explains anxiety. It is, however,

> There is no one gene, life experience, or neurochemical that explains anxiety.

---

[5]Kinderman, P. (2013, January 17). Grief and anxiety are not mental illnesses. *BBC News: Health*. Retrieved from www.bbc.co.uk/news/health-20986796
[6]Jayson, S. (2013, May 12). Book blasts new version of psychiatry's bible, the *DSM*. *USA Today*. Retrieved from www.usatoday.com/story/news/nation/2013/05/12/dsm-psychiatry-mental-disorders/2150819/
[7]For more information about the *DSM* debate, read the *Psychology Today* blog post "*DSM–5* in Distress," by former *DSM* task force chair, Allen Frances, MD: www.psychologytoday.com/blog/dsm5-in-distress

List of Major Anxiety Disorders

Generalized anxiety disorder (GAD) is characterized by excessive and uncontrollable worry about everyday situations that is above and beyond what would be expected. People with GAD tend to worry about finances, health, family, work, the future, and myriad other things.

Panic disorder involves recurring panic attacks, which are short periods of intense feelings of fear and apprehension and a variety of physical symptoms, such as racing heart, sweating, and trembling. Generally, the symptoms come out of nowhere, and even though it may seem like some specific threat is looming, there isn't one.

Agoraphobia is characterized by anxiety in situations where the person feels he or she can't escape. There is an intense fear that the person will "lose it," "freak out," or "go crazy" in public and become trapped. Consequently, the person avoids going out in public. In extreme cases, the person may become homebound.

Specific phobia is the excessive and highly distressing fear of specific objects or situations. The person avoids the objects or situations at all costs as a way to fend off the associated distress. Common examples include fear of flying, heights, snakes, spiders, and blood/needles.

Obsessive–compulsive disorder (OCD) is characterized by recurring intrusive and unremitting thoughts that produce discomfort, worry, or fear and/or compulsions (hand washing, counting, checking) that are engaged in for the purpose of reducing discomfort. Attempts at controlling or suppressing the obsessions or compulsions are generally unsuccessful.

Posttraumatic stress disorder (PTSD) develops after exposure to a traumatic event, such as rape, combat, or witnessing harm to another person. Symptoms include reexperiencing the trauma through nightmares, avoidance of reminders of the trauma, sleep disturbances, and being easily startled.

Social phobia, also referred to as social anxiety disorder, is a persistent and excessive fear of situations that may involve scrutiny or judgment by others, such as parties and other social events. Generally, there is a strong fear by the person that he or she will be embarrassed in front of others.

primarily a combination of three things: biology, environment, and psychology.

Biology

Anxiety is hardwired into humans' physiology and for understandable reasons. As we trekked across our largely unexplored planet thousands of years ago, we did it alongside a variety of threats. We shared our space with hungry and vicious animals, inhospitable fellow humans, and climates that would stress even today's most prepared hikers. Without an internal warning system, early humans would have likely been faced with extinction. Luckily, the *fight-or-flight system* came to be.

The fight-or-flight system is an extremely complex, highly sensitive, and intricately balanced biological process. Prompted by a cascade of chemicals and electrical impulses, our body prepares for one of two actions when faced by a perceived threat: defend against the threat or run away. When this happens, a variety of adaptive processes occur. The heart pumps blood to the muscles faster, which provides the increased nutrients needed to duke it out or split. Our vision narrows to focus better on the threat so that we don't get distracted by unimportant stimuli around us. And breathing becomes deeper and more frequent to deliver increased oxygen to the system. Once the threat is gone, however, or at least when we believe it is gone, an opposite process occurs in which the body regains its balance.

The fight-or-flight system has been encrypted into humans' genes and passed down from generation to generation. Unfortunately, the system's biological software has not been updated for the modern world. For some people, the alarm goes off in the absence of a real threat (e.g., seeing a snake behind the glass at the zoo) or for no apparent reason at all. The fight-or-flight system is discussed in more detail later in Chapter 8.

Our brain structures, and the chemicals that keep them functioning, also play critical roles in anxiety. The primary inhibitory neurotransmitter in the brain is gamma-aminobutyric acid (GABA), which determines how excited or relaxed we are. Too little GABA leads to anxiety, and too much GABA creates an overly relaxed state. Other important chemicals associated with anxiety are serotonin and norepinephrine. These are the chemicals that are targeted when treating anxiety with medications.

The almond-shaped amygdala is a structure in the brain that is responsible for memory, particularly memories that are emotionally charged. When you are confronted with a fearful situation, this small grouping of cells will store the event for future use, whether you want it to or not. The locus coeruleus is another important brain structure related to anxiety. In addition to being involved with sleep, it plays a key role in the development and maintenance of stress and panic.

If you find yourself thinking, "He sure didn't have much to say about the neurology of anxiety," it's because I purposely kept it brief. In my experience working with people dealing with anxiety, I generally haven't found them to be all that interested in the topic. But if you are one of those people who'd like more explanation about how the brain contributes to anxiety, you should visit the Brain and Behavior Research Foundation at http://www.bbrfoundation.org/anxiety.

Environment

There is a great deal of truth to the old saying "You are a product of your environment." Your early childhood experiences within your family, school, and with friends have as much to do with who you are today as any chemical or part of the brain. Take parenting, for example. Parents who are overly critical, neglectful, rejecting, or too protective can inadvertently create anxiety for their child. Children who grow up in homes where one or both parents have frequent and intense mood swings learn to "walk on eggshells" so as not to accidentally "cause" the next outburst. Then there are early experiences outside the home. Children who are repeatedly bullied by other kids learn to view the world as a hostile and dangerous place. Perfectionistic teachers or other authority figures model obsessive behavior and set expectations, which often cannot be achieved. And childhood abuse and trauma, which can occur within or outside of the home, can cripple a child emotionally. All these situations carry into adulthood and can lead to lifelong anxiety.

Your current environment also contributes to your anxiety. If you're under tight deadlines at work or having money problems, then you are likely anxious. If your relationship is on the rocks, or if you're concerned that you'll never find the "right" person, then you are likely anxious. If you are dealing with a sick parent or child, then you are likely anxious. I could go on for pages, but my main point is that life continually throws relationship, work, family, and social challenges your way. To varying degrees, each and every one adds to your anxiety. And without a break from the chronic stress, your body and mind will suffer the consequences.

Psychology

The psychology of anxiety is relatively simple. How you perceive, interpret, and label people, situations, events, and, well, pretty much everything else, greatly contributes to your anxiety. For example, two mothers get home after a hard day at the office; both have the same voicemail on their answering machines: "This is Ms. Smith, Johnny's teacher from school. Please give me a call when you can. I'd like to talk with you about your son." Knowing that Johnny has been working extra hard at school, the first mother becomes happy and excited. She is convinced that Ms. Smith is calling to say how hard Johnny's been working and that his grades are improving. The second mother is immediately overcome with a sense of worry and dread. She believes the only reason Ms. Smith could be calling is to tell her that Johnny's grades are getting worse. And if that's not enough, he will have to be held back a grade.

> How you perceive, interpret, and label people, situations, and events contributes to your anxiety.

As you can see, the same situation elicits two different emotional responses. The only difference is how the mothers interpret the little information available to them. One mother put a positive spin on the message, whereas the other took the negative route. Both outcomes are tied to the way the mothers thought about the situation. But, to be fair to the second mother and to make a point, worry can be adaptive. The second mother's immediate sense of worry also serves as a gentle reminder that Johnny has a tendency to let his grades slip and that she needs to maintain a constant state of concern and awareness about his progress.

A concept related to the example above is cognitive distortions. Simply put, *cognitive distortions* are exaggerated thoughts that are often not supported by evidence. They are ways in which

> Worry can be adaptive.

we convince ourselves to believe something when it is not necessarily true. They are products of our past experiences, current situations, personality, and probably a bit of biology. And they are generally lifelong patterns of thinking and are very difficult to give up. These distorted thinking patterns are related to how we feel and behave and many are directly tied to the development and maintenance of anxiety. I discuss cognitive distortions in more detail in Chapter 4.

WHO IS THIS BOOK FOR?

Everyone deals with stress and anxiety. It's part of our evolutionary and cultural makeup, and at times, we all have periods when our stress and anxiety levels go up. So in that sense, this book is for everyone. What everyone doesn't have is a clear understanding of how, when, and why anxiety becomes problematic. This book will help you gain an awareness of the many techniques available to help manage the more troubling aspects of this normal and ever-present biological, psychological, and sociological phenomenon.

This book focuses on anxiety in adults. If you are concerned about a child in your life who may be struggling with anxiety or a related mental health issue, some of the information in this book will be pertinent and some may not be. For more information on children with anxiety, I recommend *How to Find Mental Health Care for Your Child* by Ellen Braaten.[8] Likewise, if you are an older adult or are considering buying this book for friend who is an older adult, you should be aware that various conditions specific to aging and anxiety (e.g., retirement from work, memory loss and dementia, physical limitations, loss of peers and loved ones to death) are not covered in the case examples. Consider checking out the American Psychological Association's (APA's) Public Interest Office on Aging resources for information on anxiety specific to older adults (http:// www.apa.org/pi/aging/index.aspx).

HOW IS THIS BOOK DIFFERENT?

Walk into any bookstore and you'll find an aisle of self-help books a mile long. Within seconds, you'll be bombarded with promises to eliminate your depression in 14 days, tips on choosing the right mate, and how to overcome your addiction without even leaving your house. In our fast-paced, give-it-to-me-now culture, we want everything to be simple, quick, and effortless. However, this approach doesn't always work, especially when dealing with extreme levels of anxiety, depression, or whatever may be bothering

---

[8]Braaten, E. B. (2010). *How to find mental health care for your child.* Washington, DC: American Psychological Association.

you. Don't get me wrong—much of the advice you'll find in self-help books at your neighborhood bookstore can be useful. The problem is that most people read the book once, experience some immediate relief, but then put it on the shelf and forget about it. Days later, when the initial positive effects wear off, the person becomes frustrated because he or she is still having problems.

This book will help you gain a clearer understanding of what anxiety is and why it occurs. These are important aspects of change; however, this is not enough. Rarely does knowledge in itself lead to new behavior, decreased distress, or a new outlook on life. Only when knowledge is paired with concrete and proven methods for change will your life improve. This book focuses on the latter by providing tips and techniques based on proven psychological methods. Last, and possibly most important, this book orients you to the fact that anxiety is normal, expected, and often adaptive.

HOW THIS BOOK IS ORGANIZED

This book has 11 chapters. The first seven chapters take you through various coping strategies for anxiety that focus on your mind, then your body, and then your environment. Later chapters offer specific information to target more specific issues of fear and panic.

- In Chapter 1, I discuss the important role thoughts play in creating and maintaining your anxiety and provide a number of proven strategies for changing your anxiety-producing thought patterns.
- Chapter 2 covers simple techniques you can use, such as thought stopping and distraction, to manage excessive worry.
- Chapter 3 describes the art and science behind mindfulness—the ability to accept thoughts and feelings without passing judgment—and how a variety of mindfulness-based exercises can help keep your anxiety in check.

- In Chapter 4, I compare the body with a machine and emphasize how regular maintenance and care ensures its proper functioning, including healthy calibration of anxiety.
- In Chapter 5, I discuss exercise, one of the oldest and most effective methods for reducing anxiety,
- Chapter 6 details a variety of relaxation exercises for calming both the mind and body.
- In Chapter 7, I discuss how the fast-paced nature of modern society leads to much of our emotional distress, and I provide tips for how you can better manage your environment.
- Chapters 8 and 9 deal with how to manage the related concepts of fear and panic.
- In Chapter 10, I provide advice on when to seek professional help and how to best prepare for that first session with a mental health professional, whether you are seeking psychotherapy or medication services.
- In the final chapter, Chapter 11, I list a year's worth of tips and quotations to help keep you focused on your goal of managing your anxiety.

These forms are also available for download from the APA website, at http://pubs.apa.org/books/supp/moore. The forms will help guide you in creating workable systems for managing your anxiety.

GETTING THE MOST OUT OF THIS BOOK

Yes, this is a self-help book. It is designed to provide you with practical information, advice, and strategies for managing your anxiety. However, this is not the "1 . . . 2 . . . 3 . . . you're cured" variety of self-help book. First, you don't need to "cure" yourself from your anxiety. And second, even if you wanted to, simply reading a book isn't going to do it. You'll get the most out of this book if you try out its suggestions and apply them to your life. I don't recommend completing every checklist and every log and planner in the book all at once—that would be overwhelming. Instead, take an incremental approach, trying just one trick or coping tool at a time. If it works for you, try another one. If that one fails, try something else and come back to the hard one later—maybe it will be easier when you try it a second time. Keep this book on your nightstand or kitchen table, or in your work bag or backpack. This is a tool for your life, not something to read once and shelve forever after.

HOW TO USE THIS BOOK

After reading this Introduction, feel free to jump around among chapters on topics that are of greater interest and usefulness to you. However, I encourage you to glance through all of the chapters in order at least once before you do. You may find useful tips and tools in chapters you may have otherwise missed. To maximize your success at managing your anxiety, I recommend you read each chapter carefully to ensure that no stone goes unturned in your search for ways to minimize the impact anxiety has on your life.

I hope you find this book helpful. Remember, anxiety is a part of who we are, and to ignore it would be to ignore a core aspect of our psychological makeup. However, if left unmanaged during difficult times, anxiety has the potential to wreak havoc. There are no secret tricks or magic pills to rid yourself of anxiety. And as I've already mentioned, you wouldn't want to rid yourself of anxiety, even if you could. So, sit back, read at a comfortable pace, and most important, relax.

I CAN'T CONTROL THE WAY MY BRAIN WORKS, CAN I?

The world as we have created it is a process of our thinking. It cannot be changed without changing our thinking.
—Albert Einstein

The Greek philosopher Epictetus once said, "It's not what happens to you, but how you react to it that matters." Unbeknown to Epictetus, his comment underscored an important tenet of modern day psychotherapy, and cognitive therapy in particular: Regardless of what challenges life throws at you, you are in control of how you think, feel, and behave.

> You are in control of how you think, feel, and behave.

Cognitive therapy is the most widely practiced and popular form of psychotherapy today. Its theoretical foundation is based on a slight alteration of Epictetus's quote—it's not what happens to you, but how you think about what happens to you that matters. In essence, how you think about a situation or event influences how you feel about it. This in turn impacts how you behave. Following is a visual that may help you better understand the point.

Think back to the example in the Introduction of the two mothers who got the same call from their son's teacher: "This is Mrs. Smith, Johnny's teacher from school. Please give me a call when you can. I'd like to talk with you about your son." Both mothers

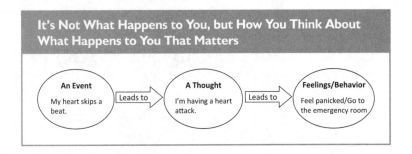

received the same general message, but one became upset ("My son is failing"), whereas the other became excited ("The teacher has noticed how hard Johnny has been working"). The difference between the two is directly related to what the mothers said to themselves. This *self-talk* will also influence the actions they take. The upset mother may avoid calling the teacher back, or she may call the principal and complain about how Johnny's problems are caused by the teacher's inexperience. The excited mother may thank the teacher for all of the time and attention she provided to Johnny and boast how hard he has been working to improve in his classes. Notice that we don't know the reality of the situation, only the mothers' interpretations.

Cognitive therapy is popular with therapists and patients because it's a practical, relatively quick, and solution-oriented way of solving many of life's problems. This is in stark contrast to popular portrayals of psychotherapy as a multiyear endeavor in which you spend countless hours on a couch while a psychiatrist analyzes your every statement and thought. Through teaching methods of modifying dysfunctional beliefs and distorted thinking patterns, therapists help patients learn to think, feel, and react in more adaptive ways. A key component of this process is identifying and overcoming what are called *cognitive distortions* (also known as *cognitive errors*). Cognitive distortions are unhelpful and often inaccurate self-defeating thoughts or self-statements that occur outside your conscious awareness. They are automatic and happen without your knowing it. And even though these automatic thoughts are often not based in reality, you accept them as truth. They lead to a variety of psychological problems, including anxiety, and are very resistant to change. Two of the more common cognitive distortions related to anxiety are *catastrophizing* (expecting the worst) and *overgeneralization* (because something bad happened in one situation, it will happen in all situations).

The connection between cognitive distortions and anxiety is straightforward and easy to understand. If you see the world and others as dangerous, then you will be anxious. If you view yourself as weak, defenseless, or inadequate, then you will be anxious. If you blow things out of proportion and make situations worse than they are, then you will be anxious. Therefore, to reduce your anxiety, you need to start thinking differently. This is where you can train yourself to think in more realistic ways. You can reduce your anxiety by recognizing and countering those thoughts that make you anxious. Keep reading to learn how.

WHERE DO COGNITIVE DISTORTIONS COME FROM?

Cognitive distortions generally develop in childhood. As a child, you do your best to make sense of the enormous, confusing, and difficult world in which you find yourself. This is normal. The problem is that your experience with the world is limited. Your assumptions are naive. You misinterpret situations, events, and the actions of others. You jump to conclusions and attribute causality to things when there is none. It's not your fault—your childhood self just doesn't know any better. But that's not all: You also learn these same things from your parents, teachers, siblings, peers, and other important people in your life. And you carry your experiences from childhood with you into adulthood. Take the case of Brynda.

Brynda grew up in a chaotic home. Her father drank a lot, and her mother was plagued by depression and anxiety. Her mother and father fought constantly. At a young age, Brynda noticed that her parents only seemed to fight when she was around. As a result, she developed the belief that her parents must fight because of her. "It must be something about me or something I do that makes them so angry at each other," she thought. She certainly believed she had solid evidence to support her belief. As soon as she walked into the home after school, she would find them arguing. She never heard of them fighting while she was at school, and they didn't seem to fight when their church pastor stopped by for a visit.

Brynda also developed the beliefs that people are unpredictable and that it's best to walk on eggshells because you can never tell what will make someone upset. Brynda vividly remembers an example that supports her belief. One Saturday afternoon, she left her tricycle outside during a rainstorm. Brynda's mother was furious. She went on and on about how irresponsible, dim-witted, and careless Brynda was. However, just a few days earlier, Brynda had accidentally broken her mother's most prized piece of china—the very piece that Brynda had been warned at least once a week since she was born not to touch. Her mother said nothing other than "things like this happen." Brynda was confused about why her mother would get so upset about the tricycle but not about the china. "Surely everyone must be like this," she thought.

Even though Brynda's childhood logic was flawed, she hung onto it as an adult. It had profound effects on her marriage and with her children. Anytime she and her husband had an argument, she always assumed it was her fault. Even after minor disagreements, she felt sick to her stomach, knowing that there was some inherent flaw with her that caused people to get upset so easily. The same was true for her children. Any disagreements with them were somehow her fault. She was also a nervous wreck not knowing when the next family fight would erupt. Her past experiences taught her that it's pointless to try and figure out how people will behave from day to day. She hated living this way.

Brynda's case illustrates how cognitive distortions develop in formative years and attach themselves for the short ride to adulthood. If left unchallenged, these distortions can lead to considerable emotional turmoil.

COMMON DISTORTIONS

The concept of cognitive distortions was developed by psychiatrist Aaron Beck,[1] popularized by psychiatrist David Burns,[2] and expanded on by psychologist Judith Beck.[3] The concept is not just theoretical—a number of studies have clearly documented cognitive distortions in thinking patterns of people with anxiety, depression, substance abuse, and a variety of other psychological conditions. The truth is that we all use one or more of these cognitive errors on a regular basis. The difference between someone who experiences distress versus someone who does not depends on the *degree of use* and the depth of which one believes them to be true. Below I discuss the 12 most commonly used cognitive distortions and provide real-world examples and specific self-statements associated with each. As you read through the list, notice how some are similar and overlap. You may need to reread them several times to appreciate the subtle differences. It will also help to come up with your own examples and self-statements while you read through them.

---

[1]Beck, A. T. (1976). *Cognitive therapies and emotional disorders.* New York, NY: New American Library.
[2]Burns, D. D. (1980). *Feeling good: The new mood therapy.* New York, NY: New American Library.
[3]Beck, J. S. (1995). *Cognitive behavior therapy: Basics and beyond.* New York, NY: Guilford Press.

Catastrophizing

Catastrophic thinking is very common in people who suffer from panic attacks.

People who engage in *catastrophic thinking* believe that the worst will happen, no matter what the circumstances of the situation may be. *Catastrophizing* is also referred to as *fortune telling*, highlighting the idea that the person somehow has the special ability to predict future events. Catastrophic thinking is very common in people who suffer from panic attacks. People who consistently engage in catastrophic thinking are often seen as dramatic, highly emotional, and fearful.

An example of catastrophic thinking goes like this: Wayne became distraught after failing his real estate licensing exam. He became convinced that he didn't have what it takes to become a real estate agent. Even though he could take the exam over as many times as he needed to, he was certain he was in over his head. Consequently, Wayne couldn't sleep at night because he became consumed by thoughts about his career. And although he had been free from panic attacks for years, he began having them again. He was on the verge of giving up his dream of becoming a real estate agent and going back to a job he hated. Life was becoming unbearable.

Self-statements that Wayne made when catastrophizing were as follows: "What if I don't become a success?" "What if I take the exam again and fail?" "I let my family down and will not be able to support them like I want to."

Overgeneralization

Overgeneralization occurs when a person views an event, behavior, or piece of information as evidence of an ongoing and never-ending pattern. The underlying belief is that if something bad happens once, then it will surely happen again. People who overgeneralize are often viewed as being "worry warts" and pessimistic.

Consider, for example, the case of Keith, who stumbled over his words a few times during an important presentation to his boss. This was the first time something like this had occurred. After the presentation, he went back to his office and ruminated about why and how this could have happened. Even though no one said anything, he was sure they laughed at him after he left the meeting. Over the next few days he became convinced that this would happen in next week's presentation. His anxiety grew each day, even to the point of having several mild panic attacks.

Keith's self-statements included, for example, "Next week's meeting is more important than this one and I'm going to screw it up," "My boss is going to fire me," and "I just know they laughed at me when I walked out."

Black-or-White Thinking

Also referred to as *polarized* and *all-or-none thinking*, this cognitive distortion is based on viewing situations as *either–or*. There are no shades of gray. It's yes or no, left or right, or black or white. The person is either a total success or utter failure. Individuals who use black-or-white thinking tend to paint themselves into corners by limiting solutions to their problems. They are often labeled as stubborn, rigid, and unwavering.

For example, Matthew recently met a nice woman who had all the qualities he was looking for in a mate . . . except one. He believed that he should only marry a woman who had graduated from college, and she had not. Even though she was smart, attractive, funny, and successful as a retail store manager, he could not get past the fact that she was not a college graduate. For Matthew, there was no wiggle room for this one self-imposed relationship requirement. He began to obsess that he would never find the perfect woman to spend the rest of his life with.

Matthew's self-statements: "I must marry a woman who graduated from college," "I can only marry a woman who meets all of my requirements," "I will not settle for anything less than perfect," and "I am destined to be alone because my standards are so high."

Personalization

The tendency to blame other people's negatives actions, comments, thoughts, and behaviors on something you did or didn't do is *personalization*. Individuals who engage in this type of cognitive distortion often blame themselves for events over which they have no control. These individuals are often labeled as self-centered, neurotic, and as having low self-esteem.

An example of this follows. Taara had just moved to a new area and desperately wanted to meet new people and make new friends. The previous week, at a party, she met Eric. They shared many similar interests and had a similar background, including attending the same elementary school. In Taara's eyes, the encounter went well, and she was sure she had found her first friend in the area. However, after several phone calls to Eric went unreturned, Taara began to blame herself for his not calling back. She became upset at the prospect of not making friends and feared she would grow old alone. She became so nervous about meeting new people that she stopped attending social functions and avoided conversations with potential friends at work.

Taara's self-statements included "He must have picked up on my desperation to make new friends," "I must have said something to offend him," and "I will never make any new friends and will spend the rest of my life alone."

Filtering

Filtering is the mental process of focusing on the negative while discounting the positive. Even if the positives greatly outweigh the negatives, the tendency to cloud one's vision with the bleakest aspect of the situation remains strong. No amount of evidence or attempts at convincing the person otherwise will make much of a difference. An individual who engages in filtering may be seen as overly self-critical.

Consider Jacob, who had been a stellar employee with his company for the previous 7 years. His recent job performance review was very positive overall. He received top marks for his abilities, hard work, communication style, professionalism, and flexibility. However, Jacob could not get over the one comment from his boss recommending he take more initiative in seeking out projects of more complexity. Jacob was sure his boss was unhappy with his performance. Why else would he make that comment? He was fearful that he would be fired and purposely avoided his boss when possible. He couldn't eat or sleep for thinking about how he would support his family if he lost his job. He started drinking more to deal with his anxiety.

Jacob's self-statements: "I knew I couldn't do well at this job," "It's only a matter of time before I'm fired," and "I will never make partner in the company."

Labeling/Mislabeling

Labeling is merely an excessive form of overgeneralization. The individual places a narrow, unshakeable, global label on himself, herself, or others when something happens that is perceived as bad. An individual who engages in labeling/mislabeling is seen as angry, bitter, and judgmental. The person is constantly worried about the behavior of others and is sensitive to any perceived personal shortcomings.

For example, Jennifer prides herself as being a good Christian. She never misses church and regularly volunteers at the church nursery. She notices that the woman who usually sits in front of her during the morning worship service has not been attending on a consistent basis. Jennifer believes too many people in the church are hypocrites and do not live their lives as they should. She grows angry at the lady's lack of attendance. Jennifer's anger turns to sadness as she wonders why she is so tough on people. She then becomes anxious at her own hypocrisy of not living up to the values and ideals she sets for herself. She also worries that her critical attitude is noticed by others. She stops going to church.

Jennifer's self-statements: "People are such hypocrites," "I'm a failure for not being able to live up to my own standards," and "God will punish me for my thoughts."

Mind Reading

In addition to fortune telling, some people believe they have the gift of mind reading. As the term implies, *mind reading* is the belief that you know what someone else is thinking. Think about it; how many times have you told someone, "I know what you're thinking"? You have perhaps already said this at least once today. The obvious truth is that we don't possess this magical ability. A person who engages in this cognitive error is seen as impatient and arrogant.

Take, for example, the case of Joseph. He and his wife had always had a strong sex life. However, he noticed that they had been intimate only a few times over the previous 6 months. He was unsure of the reasons behind the change, but he began speculating. He imagined that she no longer loved him or no longer found him attractive. He wondered whether she was plotting to leave him or whether she loved another man. He became a nervous wreck, kicking possibilities back and forth in his head. He couldn't concentrate at work, ignored his children, and emotionally withdrew from his wife.

Joseph's self-statements:"I know what she's thinking," "I know what she's up to," "She can't fool me," and "She must think I'm stupid."

Shoulds and Musts

People who use *should* and *must* statements have a very narrow and rigid view of how they think the world, others, and they themselves should be. Their expectations are very high, and similar to black-or-white thinkers, people who use this cognitive distortion often paint themselves into a corner very easily. For example, thoughts such as "I *should* make more money this year than last" and "I *must never* lose to my brother at chess" do not leave a lot of room for error. Consequently, the anxiety associated with always needing to do better or more can be intense. These individuals are seen as high achievers and worriers.

In the example for *should*s and *must*s, Ashley had always been a hard worker. She attributed this to her childhood, in which her parents (both of whom were very successful) set high expectations. Graduating from law school 3 years ago, marrying 2 years ago, and having her first child 4 months ago, she was feeling the strain of juggling a career and family. She had considered cutting back on her hours at the office, and her husband was supportive of the idea. However, she felt compelled to continue to work full-time while taking care of the family. She heard the voice of her mother saying that a woman should be able to work and take care of a family at the same time. This is what her mother did, so why shouldn't she, Ashley, be able to do the same? Ashley felt that she must follow in her mother's footsteps. She became more and more stressed and feared she would fail as a lawyer and as a mother.

She began having panic attacks and didn't want to leave the house anymore.

Ashley's self-statements: "I should be able to do it all"; "I must be perfect"; "I should put my work and family before my own health"; and "I must succeed, or I am a failure."

Control Fallacy

In the *control fallacy*, a person attributes the cause of his or her mistakes, shortcomings, and feelings of inadequacies to others. The person sees himself or herself as a helpless victim of circumstance. These individuals are often seen as helpless, self-centered, and blaming of others.

Consider, for example, Marie, who drove home from the annual office holiday party after having a few drinks. She was pulled over by the police and arrested for driving under the influence of alcohol. Marie complained that it wasn't her fault that she was drinking and driving. Her boss had ended the party earlier than expected, and she hadn't had time to sober up. She also complained that her friend Lamar, who was supposed to drive her home, left with a girl he met at the bar. Marie felt like her life was spinning out of control and that she had no power to make her situation better. She was always worrying about what life was going to throw at her next.

Marie's self-statements: "I can't control anything," "I am a victim," "It's not my fault," and "Other people are responsible for my misfortune."

OVERCOMING COGNITIVE DISTORTIONS

The first step in overcoming cognitive distortions is to realize when you are doing them. Once you gain awareness of your self-defeating thoughts, you'll be able to identify particular patterns in your thinking and begin the process of correcting them. You will likely notice that you make some errors more than others and that some have a greater impact on your anxiety. The best way to gain awareness of how your thoughts influence your anxiety and behavior is to keep a thought record. A *Thought Record*, or *Thought Log*, is simply a one-page log that enables you to track self-statements, feelings, behaviors, and situations or events that contribute to your anxiety. It also allows you to see what types of cognitive distortions you make: Are you more of a catastroph-izer or a mind reader? Do you overgeneralize or personalize? Do you engage in only one or two types of distortions or in most of them? I've provided an example to get you started. I've also included blank records at http://pubs.apa.org/books/supp/moore so you can track your thoughts over several days.

Here is how to use the Thought Log. Over the next week, each time you find yourself feeling anxious, write down your negative automatic thoughts, cognitive distortions, associated feelings and behaviors, and a realistic appraisal that counters your automatic thought. The goal is to develop greater awareness of your nega-tive self-statements and cognitive distortions that may be fueling your anxiety and other negative emotions. The Thought Log also enables you to make a more realistic appraisal of what happened, which can reduce your anxiety by giving you a clearer perspective on things.

Once you've become familiar with the types of cognitive dis-tortions you use, it's time to rely on some basic techniques to over-come them. Below are eight simple and effective ways to challenge your self-defeating thoughts and better manage your anxiety. Some techniques are better suited for specific types of cognitive distor-tions, but you will find that most can be used for several types of the most common thinking errors.

Thought Log Example

Common Distortions	What Happened?	Self-statement	Feelings	Behavior	Realistic appraisal
Catastrophizing Overgeneralization Black/White Thinking	1. Missed a deadline at work.	a. Identify the negative automatic thought: "My boss is going to fire me." b. Using the list to the left, identify what type of cognitive distortion the automatic thought is: **Catastrophizing**	Fearful	Went home sick.	"I'm a good employee. I made one mistake. It's not the end of the world."
Personalization Filtering Labeling/Mislabeling Mind Reading	2. My wife said she'd like me to do more around the house.	a. Identify the negative automatic thought: "My wife thinks I'm lazy." b. Using the list to the left, identify what type of cognitive distortion the automatic thought is: **Mind Reading**	Angry and unappreciated	Yelled at my wife.	"My wife appreciates how hard I work, but she needs extra help with the kids at times."
Shoulds and Musts Control Fallacy	3.	a. Identify the negative automatic thought: b. Using the list to the left, identify what type of cognitive distortion the automatic thought is:			

What If Technique

Also called *decatastrophizing*, the *What if* technique involves evaluating whether you are overestimating the potentially dire nature of a situation. In other words, are you assuming the worst will happen? By asking questions such as "What is the worst thing that can happen?" or "If it does occur, what would I do?" you can realistically confront your fear and even work on solving the problem if the worst does occur. In essence, by confronting the fear, you increase your level of control, which in turn reduces your anxiety.

This technique does not make the problem go away. It does, however, open your eyes to different solutions and help you realize that even though things may be tough, you will survive. At times, all we need is a little realistic perspective, and this technique can provide you that perspective. To help you master the technique, see the following example of a *What If* Technique Log; you can find blank copies at http://pubs.apa.org/books/supp/moore. The log is very simple to fill out. In the first block, write down what your overall fear is. The second block consists of the actual *What if* statement. In the third block, provide a realistic appraisal of what you would do if the feared situation actually happened. And the final block asks you to rate how strongly you believe your appraisal. If you find that your rating is below 5, your appraisal may not be all that realistic.

Reattribution

There is wisdom in the saying "There's enough blame to go around." *Reattribution* enables you to share the responsibility of a particular problem with other people or circumstances. It's very helpful for those who engage in personalization (blaming oneself for other people's negative emotions, thoughts, or behaviors). Instead of saying, "It's all my fault," ask yourself, "What other factors contributed to my current situation?" Rarely is a single person responsible for everything

The *What If* Technique Log

Fear	What if statement	How would you handle it?	Strength of belief (1–10)
My husband will leave me and I will fall to pieces.	What if my husband leaves me—What will happen to me?	I would rely on my family and friends to get me through. I would probably start dating again. It would be hard, but I would survive.	8
My children will blame me for the divorce.	What if my children tell me that it was my fault their dad left—What will I do?	I would acknowledge my children's feelings and not get angry, as they are just feelings. I would explain to them how the divorce was a mutual decision between their dad and me. I would reassure them that their dad will continue to be an important part of their lives.	7

that goes wrong. This might be the case if we lived in a vacuum, but we don't. Moreover, there are circumstances over which people have little or no control. With that being said, it's important to keep in mind that this is not an attempt to be Pollyannaish or naive. You are not pretending that the world is perfect or denying all responsibility for your actions or lack of actions; instead, you are looking for the middle

Example of Reattribution

Situation	Self-blaming statement	Reattribution
My husband was angry because he didn't have any clean shirts for work.	1. If I were a good wife, I would have known that he was getting low on clean shirts. 2. It is my fault that he is angry and if he ends up drinking too much tonight.	1. He usually tells me when he is low on clean shirts. 2. He needs to share in the responsibility of dropping off the dry cleaning. 3. If he drinks too much, that is his choice. 4. His anger has more to do with his boss and not me or the dry cleaning.

ground or gray area that most of life falls within. Chances are this is the same advice you would give to a friend who was shouldering the lion's share of blame for something that you could clearly see was not entirely his or her fault. Give yourself a break every now and again. Take a look at the Example of Reattribution.

> Rarely is a single person responsible for everything that goes wrong.

Questioning the Evidence

Humans have the uncanny ability to accept fiction for fact. We assume things to be true on the basis of speculation, incomplete information, and gut feelings. The truth is that we often draw conclusions and form opinions that are incorrect. Consequently, our feelings and actions are being supported by faulty information, which contributes to our anxiety and stress levels. What's the solution? Well, sometimes you just need to be a good detective. You need to ask yourself, "Are my thoughts based in fact, fiction, or both? What is the evidence to support my conclusions? How credible is the source?" Don't just accept your thoughts as true. Prove them to be true. For example, if you believe the world is a dangerous place, what evidence can you find to dispute this belief? You may ask yourself, "Have I felt safe before?" "How have I made it this far?" or "Do other people in my life feel safe?" Use the Questioning the Evidence Log to practice. The first two have been done for you. You can find a blank Questioning the Evidence Log at http://pubs.apa.org/books/supp/moore.

Exaggerated Fantasy

Taking an idea to the extreme often helps you put things into perspective. It also allows you to see how extreme your thinking becomes when you're anxious. Take Jonathan, for example. Jonathan is shy in social situations, especially when it comes to talking to women. Although he desperately wants to meet his soul mate, his fear that he will say something foolish and embarrass himself often overwhelms him. Consequently, he avoids meeting potential partners and worries that he will never get married. As part of treatment, Jonathan's therapist asks him to picture himself approaching a strange woman at a party. She then tells him to describe the most outlandish outcome he can imagine. She encourages him to let his imagination run wild. After he is done, she asks him to be more realistic and describe the most likely outcome for the same situation. Here is what Jonathan came up with for the extreme outcome:

> I approach this attractive woman and try to talk to her. She rejects my attempt. I feel so embarrassed. My face turns red and I break out in a sweat. Then the woman jumps on stage

Questioning the Evidence Log

Thought	Supporting evidence	Challenges to the evidence	Realistic statement
I'm at risk of being hurt every time I go outside.	1. I was assaulted 3 years ago. 2. A friend of mine was assaulted in the past.	1. Only one bad event happened in my entire life. 2. I have several friends who have never been assaulted. 3. The person who assaulted me is in jail.	Bad things do happen, but overall the world is safe. There are no guarantees, but chances are that nothing like this will ever happen again. I can't live in fear forever.
I'm going to have a panic attack and pass out if I go to the mall.	1. I have a history of panic attacks. 2. I do get anxious when I go out in public.	1. I've been to the mall numerous times and have never had a panic attack. 2. I've had panic attacks for the past 5 years and have never once passed out. 3. I've never heard of anyone passing out from a panic attack.	Although I do struggle with anxiety and panic, I've been very successful at managing my anxiety in public. Granted, anything is possible, but the likelihood of me actually passing out in public is extremely low. The likelihood of me even having a full blow panic attack at the mall is low as I know how to calm myself down and can leave at any time.

where the band is playing, grabs the microphone, and proceeds to tell the crowd how this loser tried to talk to her. Everyone starts laughing and pointing at me. I start crying and run toward the door. On my way out, I trip over a purse, which turns out to be hers. I stumble, hit my head, and pass out. The next thing I know, I am being evacuated from the party by a rescue helicopter. I pass out again and wake up in a psychiatric hospital, strapped to a bed.

And this is his more realistic outcome:

I approach this attractive woman and talk to her. I'm nervous and my voice trembles a bit, but I am able to say hello and ask her if she's having a good time. She responds in a friendly manner and says that she is indeed enjoying herself. I tell her my name and she tells me hers. I ask her if I can buy her a drink, and she accepts. We spend the next hour talking about our shared interests. I ask if I can call her next week, and she agrees.

After Jonathan finished describing the extreme and realistic scenarios of his interaction with the lady at the party, he couldn't help but laugh. Specifically, he was able to see the ridiculous nature of his first story. Comparing it with the realistic version allowed him to gain a more realistic view of his fears and put the potential consequences of being rejected into perspective. Subsequently, his anxiety about talking to strange women decreased. Use the Exaggerated Fantasy Log to practice. A blank Exaggerated Fantasy Log can be found at http://pubs.apa.org/books/supp/moore.

Stop "*Should*ing on Yourself"

Psychologist Albert Ellis coined the terms "*should*ing on yourself" and "musterbation" to describe the process of telling yourself that

Feared situation	Extreme outcome	Realistic outcome	Changes in perspective and feelings
I made a C on my economics exam and will not be able to get through college.	From here on out, I fail every exam I take. Consequently, I get kicked out of school. I can't get a job and can't rent an apartment because I don't have any money. I end up living on the streets. Because I am so desperate for money, I rob a liquor store. I get arrested and spend the next 20 years in jail.	I will feel discouraged for a while about making a C. However, making the C motivates me to work harder. I study more and my grades improve. Although I make a few more Cs during my time in college, overall, I do well. I eventually graduate and secure a job in my field.	*Perspective:* After reading through my extreme and realistic outcome scenarios, it seems silly how dire I made things seem just because I made a C on one exam. I have always been a good student, and a C is still a passing grade. I didn't study very hard for the exam, which is likely why I didn't do better. At times I am a bit rough on myself. *Feelings:* I feel less anxious about my future in school and career. I'm not worried so much anymore.

you have to do something or there may be serious consequences. The reality is that there are things you should do in life: You should eat, bathe, pay your bills, and so on. And if you don't do these things, there can be real consequences. However, telling yourself "I should eat healthier" or "I must not lose," especially if you beat yourself up emotionally if you don't succeed, causes anxiety.

So, where do *should*s and *must*s come from? They are carry-overs from your childhood when you were being taught right from wrong. *Should*s and *must*s are highly useful for parents when teaching their children what is appropriate or how to be safe. Parental statements such as "You should not hit others," "You should share with your friends," "You must not run out into the street," and "You must not touch the stove" are all pieces of sound advice for children. And if one of the parental commandments is broken, there may be consequences (time out, loss of privileges, pain/injury). The problem is that once people learn the difference between right and wrong, *should*s and *must*s aren't all that useful. In fact, they imply certain expectations related to feelings and behaviors, such as "I shouldn't feel this way" or "I must give in or things will get worse." Moreover, these expectations are often unrealistic, such as "I must be the best parent ever" or "I should always be first." These unrealistic expectations inevitably lead to anxiety.

Instead of painting yourself into a corner with *should*s and *must*s, give yourself some wiggle room. Use statements such as "It would be nice to eat healthier," "I would like to win," and "I will do my best to succeed." It may seem like semantics, but what you say to yourself really does have a tremendous effect on how you feel. The best way to get a handle on your *should*s and *must*s is to catch yourself using them and replace them with less demanding alternative words and phrases. See the example in

> Give yourself some wiggle room.

Shoulds and **Musts** Log	
Write down any *should* or *must* statement you use during the day. Identify the potential problem the statement may cause for you.	Write down an alternative to the *should* or *must* statement. Identify how the new statement helps you.
Statement: I should not get so nervous in public.	*New statement:* I will do my best to avoid getting nervous at the mall. However, if I do, I know how to manage it.
Potential problem: I set myself up for failure because I do get nervous in public. I will feel like a failure if it happens again.	*How does it help?* It acknowledges that I struggle with being in public places and that I also know how to manage my anxiety through techniques I have learned.
Statement:	*New statement:*
Potential problem:	*How does it help?*

the *Shoulds* and *Musts* Log. You can find the blank *Should*s and *Must*s Log at http://pubs.apa.org/books/supp/moore.

Behavioral Experiment

As I mentioned earlier, don't accept your thoughts as automatic truths. Humans have the tendency to accept things on face value, without any supporting evidence. It's important to maintain a healthy skepticism. It's also important to apply real-world tests to assess the accuracy of your beliefs. For example, if you believe that driving to the store will be too anxiety provoking, try it and see. If you think you made a complete fool of yourself while delivering a speech last week, ask someone who attended the meeting how you did. If you believe that your chest pain is caused by heart problems and not anxiety, then go see a doctor. Yes, in some instances, your thoughts will be accurate. If that turns out to be the case, at least now you have evidence to support your beliefs. Instead of wondering "What if," you can start problem solving.

Following is an example of a worksheet that can help you conduct real-world experiments for the purpose of testing out the accuracy of your thoughts and beliefs. You can find a blank Behavioral Experiment worksheet at http://pubs.apa.org/books/supp/moore. Start out by choosing a thought or belief that you feel contributes to your anxiety. Next, identify an alternative to your original thought or belief, one that is less anxiety provoking. Rate them both with regard to how strongly you believe them. Note that it's expected that your alternative thought will be rated lower on how strong you believe it to be true. The next step is to set up the experiment. It may help you to answer questions such as "What would I do?" "Where would it take place?" and "When should it happen?" The more specific you can be, the better. Identify any safety behaviors that you have relied on in the past or believe you may rely on during the experiment. *Safety behaviors* are merely those behaviors people engage in to reduce their anxiety. They can be useful in managing anxiety, but they can also prevent people from experiencing anxiety, which can be important in overcoming our fears. For example, if a man who has a fear of flying always uses alcohol or medication to manage his fear before getting on a plane, he will always have a fear of flying. His safety behaviors are drinking and taking medication. Once you've identified any safety behaviors, make a list of potential problems that may occur as well as how you can overcome them. In

Behavioral Experiment Example

What is the belief or thought to be tested?	Rate how strongly you agree with this thought or belief (0-100%)

Is there an alternative, maybe one that you don't believe in as strongly?	Rate how strongly you believe in the alternative (0-100%)

What experiment could put this belief to the test?
What would you do?
Where would it take place?
When should it happen?

What safety behaviors would need to be dropped?

What problems are likely? How could they be overcome?

Outcome: What happened? What did you observe?

What have you learned? How does this affect the original belief?	Rate how strongly you agree with the original thought or belief now (0-100%)

From PsychologyTools website. Reprinted with permission.

(continues)

What is the belief or thought to be tested?	Rate how strongly you agree with this thought or belief (0-100%)
If I speak in public I will shake so much that people will notice and laugh at me	*90%*

Is there an alternative, maybe one that you don't believe in as strongly?	Rate how strongly you believe in the alternative (0-100%)
I will feel nervous and feel like I am shaking but people won't notice	*0%*

What experiment could put this belief to the test?
What would you do?
Where would it take place?
When should it happen?

Speak up at the next meeting on Monday - I could present some of the data that I have been meaning to show.
I could ask my friends if they noticed me shaking when I talk

What safety behaviors would need to be dropped?
Staying quiet
Holding on to the table

What problems are likely? How could they be overcome?

Might not get a chance to speak unless I put it on the agenda

Outcome: What happened? What did you observe?

I was really nervous and was very aware of my hands
My friends said I spoke well and that they could not see me shake

What have you learned? How does this affect the original belief?	Rate how strongly you agree with the original thought or belief now (0-100%)
Although I feel nervous when speaking it's not as obvious to other people *Belief they will laugh*	*50%*

From Psychology Tools website. Reprinted with permission.

other words, who or what could derail your experiment? You then finish up by reviewing the outcome, what you've learned from the experiment, and how the experiment affected your original belief.

Lemons to Lemonade

There is a reason sayings such as "Look for the silver lining," "When one door closes, another opens," and "Turn lemons into lemonade" are so pervasive in our culture: They are based in truth. Life is filled with crises and catastrophic events. They cause us to feel overwhelmed and helpless. However, losing a job may lead to finding a better one. A new and fulfilling marriage can start only after a bad one ends. The death of a loved one can bring you closer to those living around you. This may seem overly simplistic, but I believe there is profound meaning in these age-old truisms. Learn to look for the positives that often follow difficult times. They may not be easy to see, but they are there. Take a look at the Finding Positive Results During Times of Crisis Worksheet. You can find a blank worksheet at http://pubs. apa.org/books/supp/moore.

> Look for the positives that often follow difficult times.

Role Reversal

What would you tell a friend who is having the same negative thoughts that you're having? What advice would you give your spouse, parent, sibling, or child if they were in your situation? Take the role of counselor, advisor, or even therapist. Thinking through your problems with the perspective of helping someone else allows you to do three things. First, it provides clarity. You see things more clearly as a result of looking through a different set of lenses. Second, it highlights the often negative and distorted nature of what

Finding Positive Results During Times of Crisis Worksheet		
List something bad that has happened to you in your life.	List at least three positive things that resulted after the difficult experience.	How did this experience positively impact your life overall? For example, did you become stronger, more compassionate, less fearful?
My spouse was unfaithful and it pushed us to the brink of divorce.	1. We became more honest with each other about our relationship. 2. We rededicated our love to each other. 3. We learned to listen to each other.	I now know that I can handle a devastating event like infidelity. I have developed a greater understanding of the importance of marriage.
	1. 2. 3.	

you say to yourself. Third, it stimulates problem solving. Go ahead: Give yourself some sound advice!

SUMMARY

Thoughts are powerful. They influence how you feel and behave. But they don't have to control you. Gaining awareness of the different types of cognitive distortions and cognitive errors you make and applying some simple techniques to correct them will not only reduce your anxiety but will also create a new way of looking at the world. Here are a few points to take away from this chapter.

- It's not what happens to you, it's how you think about what happens to you that matters.
- Cognitive distortions are automatic and outside of your awareness.
- Gaining awareness of your cognitive distortions is the first step to defeating them.
- Always question the evidence of your thoughts; verify their validity.
- Catastrophizing contributes tremendously to the development and maintenance of panic.

CHAPTER 2

HOW CAN I TRAIN MY MIND NOT TO WORRY?

When I look back on all the worries, I remember the story of the old man who said on his deathbed that he had a lot of trouble in his life, most of which never happened.

—Winston Churchill

A former professor of mine once said, "A person who doesn't worry is a person who's no longer alive." Granted, the statement is a tad dramatic, but it is correct nonetheless.

> Worry allows us to make sense of our fears.

From an evolutionary psychology perspective, worry is what separates people from animals. It allows people to make sense of their fears and keeps them safe from environmental threats. There are also practical benefits to worrying. In the book *The Worry Cure: Seven Steps to Stop Worry from Stopping You*,[1] psychologist Robert Leahy notes five rational and sensible reasons why people worry. They include that worry

- helps with problem solving;
- prevents things from being overlooked;
- supports the belief that if you look long enough, you'll find a solution;
- reduces your chances of being surprised; and
- instills a sense of being responsible and active.

---

[1]Leahy, R. (2006). *The worry cure: Seven steps to stop worry from stopping you.* New York, NY: Three Rivers Press.

Indeed, worry leads people to solutions that they may have missed with only a cursory mental review. It ensures that they consider and evaluate the various nuances of the different problems life throws at them. It motivates them to persevere and rewards them for successes. It better prepares people for what's to come and reduces the number of blind spots. And it protects people's sense of self-worth, esteem, and control over their lives through purposeful and thoughtful action.

On the flipside, worry can be one's worst enemy. Left unchecked, run-of-the-mill worry can turn into *obsessive rumination*, the sustained focus on the symptoms and origins of one's distress. In other words, the person is not only dealing with future-oriented potential problems, he or she is also stuck in the past, thinking about problems that are days, months, or years old. In extreme cases, the person becomes incapacitated by worry. Work, family, and friendships suffer. It becomes easier to stay home and think about what's going wrong than to find and implement solutions. As psychologist Edmund Bourne wrote in his book *Coping With Anxiety: 10 Simple Ways to Relieve Anxiety, Fear & Worry,*[2] obsessive worry is a negative spiral that leaves the person feeling trapped and unable to change direction.

A number of physical symptoms and health complications are also associated with chronic worry. Prolonged worry causes the body to release increased levels of stress hormones. If these levels aren't reduced, the constant strain will exact a noticeable physical toll. Common physical problems include

- difficulty swallowing,
- dizziness,

---

[2]Bourne, E. (2003). *Coping with anxiety: 10 simple ways to relieve anxiety, fear & worry.* Oakland, CA: New Harbinger.

- dry mouth,
- fast heartbeat,
- heart palpitations,
- fatigue,
- headaches,
- inability to concentrate,
- irritability,
- muscle aches,
- muscle tension,
- nausea,
- restlessness,
- rapid breathing,
- shortness of breath,
- sweating,
- trembling and twitching,
- compromised immune system,
- digestive disorders,
- short-term memory loss, and
- heart disease.[3]

Chronic worrying differs from regular day-to-day worrying in two important ways. First, everyday worry typically only lasts for a short period of time. For example, if you're anxious about an upcoming exam, the anxiety will go away once the exam is over. In contrast, a chronic worrier will worry about the next test, the next class, graduation, career, and so on. Second, everyday worry generally has little impact on your day-to-day life. Sure, you may have a hard time concentrating in a meeting if you're worried about how

---

[3]WebMD. *How worrying affects the body.* Retrieved from http://www. webmd.com/balance/guide/how-worrying-affects-your-body?page=2

Everyday worry typically only lasts a short period of time.

you'll pay for the furnace that just went out, but you can still get your job done. A chronic worrier is not so lucky. He or she will miss deadlines and meetings, forget to pick up the kids from school or soccer practice, or drop the ball on important projects. The good news is that the vicious cycle of worry can be broken with a few simple techniques. But, as with all techniques in this book, a conscious and sustained effort is required to reap the benefits.

DIFFERENT FORMS OF WORRY

Worry takes on many shapes and forms. The purpose and extent of the worry are unique to the individual. However, there are commonalities in how and why people worry. Three common forms of worry are *general worry*, *obsessive worry*, and *social worry*.

General Worry

As I mentioned above, we all worry about something from time to time. We stress about bills, school, relationships, our job, and any number of other typical life hassles. The general worrier, or what I call the equal opportunity worrier, worries about multiple problems all the time. The worry is excessive, seemingly uncontrollable, and often not backed up by any evidence. The late prominent psychologist Albert Ellis referred to the latter as *irrational beliefs*. (I avoid using this term, as it can be seen as judgmental and minimizes the person's distress.) Another characteristic of the general worrier is that the amount of worry is generally greater than what the actual situation deserves. This leaves the person feeling frustrated, helpless, and even "crazy." If severe enough, this type of worry is typically labeled *generalized anxiety disorder* by mental health professionals.

The focus of the worry varies from person to person. The most common themes include bills/finances/retirement, health and safety of loved ones, marriage/relationships, family problems, injury/death, and work/school. Again, it's important to remember that the worry is out of proportion to the situation that the person is worrying about and is often not based on solid facts. Worrying about finances, family, health, or work from time to time is normal. It becomes problematic when the worry interferes with normal life. Examples of this type of worry follow.

- Finances. A husband/father can't sleep at night, pays the household bills late or doesn't pay them at all, or causes conflict in the family because he constantly worries about not having enough money to buy food for his family.
- Health and safety of loved ones. A mother is so consumed with thoughts of her daughter getting sick that the child isn't allowed to leave the home or her normal social activities are severely restricted.
- Marriage/relationship. A wife constantly worries about her husband leaving her, which drives an emotional and physical wedge between them.
- Family problems. A teenager stresses daily about whether her parents will ever divorce. Consequently, she uses alcohol to relieve her anxiety.
- Injury/death. A woman worries so much about her elderly father dying that she avoids going to see him. This causes the woman to become depressed.
- Work/school. A college sophomore can't stop thinking about what type of job he will get after graduation. He is on the verge of being expelled from school because of low grades.

Obsessive Worry and Thoughts

Obsessions are unwanted repetitive and persistent thoughts, images, or impulses that cause distress for the individual having them. The thoughts are extremely difficult to resist and are usually viewed as excessive by the person. The obsessive worrier may engage in compulsive behaviors (checking and rechecking, hand washing, arranging and rearranging items) to lessen or neutralize the anxiety. These behaviors work to varying degrees, but they do not eliminate the anxious thoughts. This type of worry is typically labeled as *obsessive–compulsive disorder* by mental health professionals.

The focus of the obsessive worry varies from person to person. The most common themes include contamination; orderliness/ neatness; safety/harm; and unacceptable aggressive, sexual, or religious thoughts or impulses. As with general worry, obsessive worry is only problematic when the thoughts and associated behaviors interfere with normal life. Here are examples of this type of worry.

- Contamination. A woman obsesses about catching an illness from door handles, which causes her to no longer leave the house.
- Orderliness/neatness. A man worries constantly about his tie being crooked, so much so that he goes to the bathroom a few dozen times each day to check himself in the mirror. This has caused him to get behind on several projects at work.
- Safety/harm. A father is consumed with thoughts about something bad happening to his children if he drives even 1 mile an hour over the speed limit. He dreads driving to and from work.
- Unacceptable aggressive, sexual, or religious thoughts or impulses. A Sunday school teacher has stopped going to

church because of uncontrollable thoughts and images she has of herself engaging in sexual activity with the church's pastor.

Social Worry

Many people are uncomfortable in social situations. For some, it comes in the form of shyness at parties or other social gatherings. For others, it's about being afraid of saying something incorrect or unintentionally offending someone. In general, socially anxious people tend to worry that they will be negatively judged in some way. Consequently, they avoid social situations for fear of being criticized or embarrassed. Social worry also leads to a number of physical symptoms, which are distressing to the person. These include

- sweating,
- blushing,
- racing heart,
- dizziness,
- dry mouth,
- quivering voice,
- trembling/shaking, and
- tremulous voice.

This type of worry is typically labeled as *social phobia*, or *social anxiety disorder*, by mental health professionals.

The types of things socially anxious people worry about are limitless. However, the most common ones include the following: starting a conversation, being rejected by strangers, public speaking; meeting new people, entering a room with seated people; and making eye contact. As with general and obsessive worry, social worry is only problematic when the thoughts interfere with normal day-to-day life. Examples of the most common sources of social worry follow.

- Starting a conversation. A single, intelligent, and attractive man in his mid-30s hasn't been on a date in 2 years. He has had several opportunities just in the past month to ask a woman on a date who he knew was interested in him. His fear of talking to a relative stranger prevented him from doing so.
- Being rejected by strangers. A successful businesswoman has been unhappy with her job for the last few years. She would like to leave but has avoided going on job interviews because of her fear that she will be turned down.
- Public speaking. A nurse was recently promoted to an administrative position. One of her new responsibilities is to lead a daily information meeting each morning for the nursing staff. She has decided to resign because of her nervousness about speaking in front of the staff.
- Meeting new people. A woman in her early 50s recently divorced from her husband of 30 years. She would like to begin dating again. She doesn't, because she's afraid the men she meets will think something is wrong with her because she's divorced.
- Entering a room with seated people. An attractive young woman avoids going to restaurants because she is worried about being judged by those already in the room.
- Making eye contact. A college student avoids leaving her dorm room because she's afraid that she'll unintentionally offend someone by staring at them.

WORRY CONTROL TECHNIQUES

Now that you understand the different types of worry and how worry can affect you, it's time to learn a few techniques. The following tips are straightforward and simple. However, don't let their simplicity fool you. They are extremely effective for managing worry. But you must practice them. This is especially true for those that may not come naturally to you.

Before you start implementing the techniques below, it's important to understand that not all problems that cause you to worry have solutions. Examples include certain illnesses, natural and human-made disasters, and a variety of life circumstances and situations. Therefore, it's helpful to approach your problems based on the two major coping styles described by Lazarus and Folkman[4]—problem focused and emotion focused. *Problem-focused coping* enables you to fix or correct the problems that can be fixed or corrected, whereas *emotion-focused coping* enables you to emotionally manage those things that can't be changed (e.g., you can change the way you think about your mother's illness, but you can't change the fact that she's sick). The following techniques help you with both styles of coping.

Let Yourself Worry

Yes, that's right. I want you to worry. The catch is that you can only do it for 20 minutes at the same time each day. The problem is not that you worry. As I've said before, worry is a part of who you are. And in some situations, it's helpful. The problem is that if you are like most people, you worry haphazardly. In other words, you worry during a meeting, while taking a shower, when you're having dinner, or lying in bed while you're trying to fall asleep. There is no structure or consistency in your worry patterns. Consequently, you get behind at work or school. You're getting only 5 hours of sleep at night. And

---

[4]Lazarus, R. S., & Folkman, S. (1984) Coping and adaptation. In W. D. Gentry (Ed.), *The handbook of behavioral medicine* (pp. 282–325). New York, NY: Guilford Press.

you feel helpless and hopeless because it seems like you are overrun by worrisome thoughts.

It's time to change your pattern. Try the following steps to gain better predictability and management of your worry.

1. Create a designated worry time that lasts for 20 minutes at the same time each day. Maybe this is before you go to work or after you get home. When you worry is completely up to you. However, I don't recommend that you try this exercise within an hour of going to bed; you may find it hard to shut off your mind after 20 minutes when you first start, which could make it harder for you to fall asleep. Make sure that the place you choose is quiet and free from interruptions (leave your cell phone in the other room, turn off the television).

   Create a designated worry time.

2. Throughout the day, write down any worries that pop into your head. For example, if you're washing dishes and you start worrying about how you'll pay next month's mortgage, write it down. Then tell yourself that you'll worry about it during your designated worry time. This is one of the hardest parts of the exercise. Worrying throughout the day has become natural for you. It has become a habit. And habits can be hard to break. But with a bit of practice and patience, you will get the hang of it.

3. During your designated worry time, worry until your heart's content. Worry about whatever you want to. Pull out the slips of paper crumpled in your pocket that list all your worries from the day and worry about them. Worry, worry, and worry some more. But stop after 20 minutes. This is all you get. If there are things you still need to worry about, put them

on tomorrow's worry agenda. If you find that you don't need the full 20 minutes, find something fun to do.

The best part of this technique is that it allows you to postpone your worry. By not getting bogged down with worry during the day, you're able to focus on important things like finishing tasks at work, taking care of the children, paying bills, and so on. You still allow yourself the opportunity to worry about whatever's bothering you. You just become a more effective and efficient worrier. Don't be surprised if after a few days you find that you don't need the full 20 minutes.

Distract Yourself

The goal of distraction is simple—delay your worry long enough so that the urge to worry passes. If it comes back, you just have to delay it again. Often, just this basic act will reduce the importance of the worry and push it completely out of awareness. This technique is successfully used by people who want to stop smoking or drinking. It's also used by people on diets who need help fighting cravings to eat. The type of delay needs to be something that doesn't allow you to worry while you're doing it. For example, watching television is not a good delay tactic. It's easy for your mind to wander while you're zoned out watching reruns of your favorite sitcom. If you find yourself worrying a lot, try a few of the following activities.

- Journal/write. Writing is a great way to distract yourself from your worry. You don't need to be a professional writer to craft a short story, poem, or letter to a loved one. You can even free associate with your writing: write out whatever pops into your head. It doesn't matter how nonsensical it may seem. In fact, the more wild and strange the writing gets, the funnier it is when you go back and read it.

- Play a board game or complete a puzzle. Like most of us, you've probably forgotten how fun playing board games and putting puzzles together are. Games of strategy can be incredibly engrossing. Within a few minutes, your mind becomes focused solely on the task at hand. Any attempt at worrying become futile, as it's impossible to be fully engaged in both.
- Read. It may sound boring, especially if you don't read a lot, but similar to playing a board game or putting a puzzle together, reading allows you to fully immerse yourself into something other than your distressing thoughts.
- Pray. Prayer is an excellent way to distract yourself from worry. It brings about a sense of calmness, serenity, and peacefulness. Plus, if you are at the office, school, or the grocery store, you don't have to run home and find a puzzle or book. You just need to find somewhere you can be alone for a few minutes. Keep in mind that you don't have to be a religious person to pray. You can pray to whomever or whatever fits with your views on life, higher power, and so on.
- Play with your child. Nothing says "I'm free from worry" like playing with your child. Children have the ability to make us laugh, appreciate the small things in life, and remind us that life should be about having fun. It's hard to take yourself too seriously when you are engaging in a friendly game of hopscotch or building a mud pie.
- Be intimate with your partner. Although this can mean having sex, it could also mean simply focusing your complete attention on your partner's emotional needs. The former may present a challenge, especially if you are in public. The latter is more doable when others are around.
- Stay in the present. If you find yourself ruminating about past events or stressing over what may happen tomorrow or next week, bring your mind back to the present. *Mindfulness*, or

the ability to be aware of the things going on around you, is a great way to distract yourself. If your thoughts wander again, bring your awareness back to what's going on around you. For more information about mindfulness, see the next chapter.

- Stop your thoughts. Thought stopping is a very simple and effective way for controlling worrisome thoughts. In essence, the technique interrupts negative, biased, and distressing thoughts by consciously telling yourself to . . . you guessed it, stop! Once the thoughts are stopped in their tracks, you then replace them with more positive and realistic ones. This technique is successful for all types of worry. Those with obsessive worry find it to be particularly helpful. The following thought-stopping exercise can be practiced at home.

Thought-Stopping Exercise

1. Write down a negative thought that has been bothering you lately. Then, next to the thought, list three or four neutral or positive alternatives to that thought. An example might be "I have control of my thoughts" or "remember to stay in the present." If you have trouble coming up with less distressing alternatives, go back to Chapter 1 and review the discussion on cognitive distortions.

2. Consciously bring the negative thought into your awareness and focus on it for 20 to 30 seconds. Once the thought is running through your head on what seems like a continuous loop, shout "Stop!" If the thought continues, yell "Stop!" again. Do this until the thought is stopped dead in its tracks.

3. Now that the thought is stopped, choose one of the neutral or positive alternatives you listed before you started. Repeat this thought over and over for 2 to 3 minutes. Relax, clear your mind, and sit quietly.

4. After a minute or two, repeat Steps 2 and 3 using the original negative thought.
5. Start the process again with a different negative thought. Practice the technique until it becomes second nature.

Challenge Your Thoughts

This is more of a reminder than a technique: Practice the skills you learned in the previous chapter. Remember that your thoughts are often biased and not supported by evidence. Look for flaws in your thinking. Find evidence that disputes your negative and slanted views. Be a scientist and set up real-world experiments to test the correctness of your hypotheses. Identify a best, worst, and likely case scenario and plan for each. Figure out what benefit worrying provides. If it doesn't provide any, ask yourself why you continue to do it. But don't stop there: Once you have identified those negative thoughts, replace them with positive ones. Research by psychologist Philip Kendall has shown that emotional health is improved if we increase our ratio of positive thoughts over negative ones. In other words, for every negative thought you have, you should generate two, three, or four positive ones. For example, replace the self-statement "I'm never going to be able to decide what to do" with "I will figure things out eventually," "I've been successful at solving my problems in the past," and "it's not the end of the world if I don't decide today." Now you have a 3-to-1 ratio of positive-to-negative self-statements. If you practice this routine every time you have a negative thought, you will see your anxiety decrease over time.

Get Off the Fence

Indecisiveness is the lifeblood of worry. Anxious people have a difficult time making decisions. It may be due to fear of making the "wrong" decision or offending others, or to an inability to accept the possible consequences. Regardless of the reason, an indecisive person will remain an anxious person. Follow the seven-step decision-making process originally developed by Dr. Pam Brown so that you can get off the fence and into the yard.

1. The first step is to identify the decision. It may sound simple, but people often get stuck on Step 1. Without fully understanding what decision needs to be made, you will find yourself confused, frustrated, and eager to give up on the decision-making process. Ask yourself, "What do I want to have happen?" or "What specific question do I need answered?" You may find it helpful to write down the decision you need to make on a piece of paper and refer back to it throughout the process.

2. Next, collect information. People are really good at forming conclusions about things before all the evidence is in. We see things through our own personal prism, which is made up of our past experiences and beliefs about how the world works. However, we are not always correct. Therefore, it's important to gather as much evidence as you can so that you can make an informed decision. You may want to ask family, friends, colleagues, or even casual acquaintances what they would do if they were in your situation.

3. The third step is to identify alternatives to choose from. Once you've figured out what you need to decide and have gathered as much information as you can, you can generate a list of alternatives to choose from. The best way is to write down as many potential choices as you can conjure up. Avoid the urge to automatically dismiss or accept them. Just make a list.

4. Next, weigh the evidence. Once your list is in place, identify the various pros and cons associated with each potential choice. As you begin to review the pros and cons of the various

65

Making the Best Decision

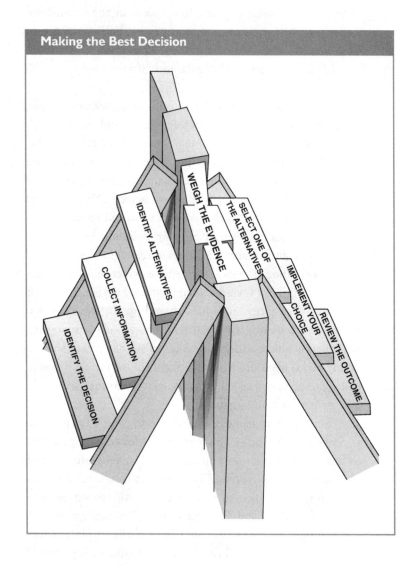

IDENTIFY THE DECISION

COLLECT INFORMATION

IDENTIFY ALTERNATIVES

WEIGH THE EVIDENCE

SELECT ONE OF THE ALTERNATIVES

IMPLEMENT YOUR CHOICE

REVIEW THE OUTCOME

alternatives, you will start to favor some over others. You may even want to assign a value for each choice ranging from 1 to 10, with 1 being the *worst* choice and 10 being the *best* choice.

5. The fifth step is to select one of the alternatives. Now it's time to choose. At this point, it's important to remember that there are few absolutes in life. There generally is no perfect answer or solution. As humans, we make choices, adapt to the choices we make, and learn from those choices that turn out to be less than stellar. If you are having a difficult time choosing between two or three seemingly good alternatives, don't be afraid to rely on your intuition. Intuition can be very accurate at times.

6. Next, implement your choice. Once you've made the selection, it's then time to implement it. Don't hesitate or delay. You've made up your mind, and it's time to act. You may find yourself getting more anxious at this point. That's okay. Acknowledge any self-doubt, fear, or worry you may have and then move forward.

7. Finally, review the outcome. The last step in the decision making process is to determine whether it was successful or not. If not, what part or parts didn't work? Can things be tweaked to enhance the outcome? What can you learn from this decision, and how would you do things differently next time? Maybe you wouldn't do anything differently. Remember not to be too harsh on yourself if it didn't work out like you expected: Expectations and reality don't always match up. Congratulate yourself for following through, adapt to the outcome, and steady yourself for the next big life decision.

Acceptance

"God grant me the serenity to accept the things I cannot change, the courage to change the things I can, and the wisdom to know

> An anxious person is someone who will not let go.

the difference." The first few sentences of the Serenity Prayer are profound. There are some things in life that people can control: how we talk to people, what we eat for dinner, how we dress, and so on. We can't control things like the weather, the devastation of war, or other people's behavior. A person free from unhealthy anxiety is a person who knows when to let go of something that he or she can't change. An anxious person is someone who, even in the face of evidence to the contrary, will not let go. Letting go will free you from your anxious thoughts. Reciting the prayer below may help.

> Please give me the wisdom to know when I should let go of those things in my life that I cannot change. Help me find the courage to face adversity when every ounce of my being says to avoid it. Grant me the strength to stay the course when my mind tries to distract me from what I know is best. Remind me that with your support, I have control over my thoughts, feelings, and actions. Bless me with the ability to accept pain and uncertainty as a part of life.

SUMMARY

Worry is common in today's society. It helps people solve problems, serves as a warning of potential threats, and reduces errors. However, left unchecked, worry can lead to chronic physical and emotional stress. There are a variety of techniques you can use to manage your worry. Here are a few points to take away from this chapter.

- Worry is part of everyday life. It only becomes a problem if it interferes with your relationships, work, school, and overall quality of life.

- Worry can be classified as general, social, or obsessive.
- Negative thoughts create and maintain worry.
- Establishing set worry times and using distractions are effective ways of managing anxiety.
- Accepting those things out of your control can free you from anxiety.

CHAPTER 3

WHAT IS MINDFULNESS?

Mindfulness is simply being aware of what is happening right now without wishing it were different; enjoying the pleasant without holding on when it changes (which it will); being with the unpleasant without fearing it will always be this way (which it won't).

—James Baraz, author and meditation teacher

Life is chaotic. You're pulled in countless directions, and you take on additional responsibilities each day. If you're not rushing to the grocery store, picking up the kids from school, or planning for tomorrow's make-or-break business meeting, you're focused on dozens of other minor tasks that have to get done. So, what's the problem? The problem is that your one and only life is passing you by. You miss the experience of day-to-day life, when you focus just on the task and not the process. In other words, you are so caught up in the end result that you've forgotten about the experience of getting there. Sure, you're daughter made an *A* on her science project, but did you notice how much she smiled while you worked on it together? Once again, you created a gourmet meal for your family, but did you appreciate the vivid colors of the vegetables or the artistic nature of your culinary masterpiece? Or, on the commute into work this morning, do you remember the face of the man who let you change lanes in front of him? Probably not. It's not your fault. It's just how fast paced we've become as a society. We've made multitasking a necessary art form. But there are consequences.

In their book *The Mindful Way Through Anxiety: Break Free From Chronic Worry and Reclaim Your Life*,[1] psychologists Susan Orsillo and Lizabeth Roemer discuss a variety of problems caused by multitasking. A few of the more salient ones are attention and memory problems, strained relationships, disconnectedness from work and loved ones, confusion, and hopelessness. Multitasking also fuels anxiety. You're always worrying about the next task. You're concerned over making careless mistakes. The stress of always being on the go is overwhelming. And the question of whether you missed precious moments with family or friends in the past is always with you. Be honest: How often do you tell yourself, "I need to slow down" or "I should spend more time with my family?" When was the last time you noticed the dress your daughter was wearing or were able to accurately describe the conversation you had with your family over dinner? Heck, when was the last time you even had dinner with your family? You see my point. If you're like most people, you are missing out on a lot.

The practice of mindfulness can help correct this pattern. *Mindfulness*, put in simple terms, is the practice of focusing your attention on the present. It's not concerned with the past or the future, only the here and now. It teaches you how to be open to new experiences while avoiding judgment, labels, and definitions. Acceptance is key. Thoughts, feelings, behaviors, and physical sensations are nothing more or less than thoughts, feelings, behaviors, and physical sensations—they just exist and are void of meaning. Consider, for example, the case of Joseph, who experiences panic attacks. A common thought that pops into his

---

[1]Orsillo, S. M., & Roemer, L. (2011). *The mindful way through anxiety: Break free from chronic worry and reclaim your life.* New York, NY: Guilford Press.

head before he has an attack is, "I'm going to lose it and pass out in front of everybody." When this thought occurs, he labels himself as "weak" and "crazy." He notices that his heart rate increases and he starts to sweat. This makes him more nervous as he associates these physical sensations with an impending attack. He looks for the nearest door and tells himself he better leave to avoid embarrassment. He leaves, his anxiety goes down, and he feels ashamed that he let anxiety get the best of him again. If Joseph used mindfulness in this type of situation, he would simply acknowledge the thought of "losing it" and avoid the negative labels of "weak" and "crazy." He would do the same for his physical sensations, as well as acknowledge and deflect his urge to leave. He would also divert his attention away from his thoughts, feelings, and sensations by focusing on his present surroundings: What other people are present? What sounds can he hear? What color are the walls and floor? What is the temperature of the room? And so on. You'll hear more about how to do this later in the chapter. But for now, just be aware that mindfulness takes focus away from your thoughts, feelings, and sensations and places it on the many details and intricacies of the here and now. And trust me—there are a lot of them.

The practice of mindfulness is not new. It's firmly rooted in the ancient religion and philosophy of Buddhism, but in fact most religions incorporate some type of mindfulness into their practice.

> Mindfulness is the practice of focusing your attention on the present.

Examples include prayer, meditation, chanting, reading and recitation of scriptures, and many other ritualistic practices. Although for some people mindfulness carries the stigma of being a "new age" practice that only "hippies" do, the truth of the matter is that mindfulness has become mainstream in the field of psychology and has a large amount of research supporting its use.[2,3] Just a few of the psychological and physical problems mindfulness is helpful for include but are not limited to the following:[4]

anxiety	stress reduction
heart disease	fibromyalgia
depression	insomnia
high blood pressure	cancer
addiction	relationship discord
chronic pain	diabetes
eating disorders	sexual problems
gastrointestinal problems	decreased immune function

Mindfulness also teaches you to be more calm and collected when faced with extremely emotional and stressful situations, compassionate and sensitive to the feelings and needs of others, and appreciative of your surroundings. In other words, it can make you a better person, the type of person others are drawn to. Although it's not a panacea or magic bullet that will take away all of your worries, fears, and stress, it is another effective tool that allows you to manage your anxiety. It just takes a bit of practice.

---

[2]Hofmann, S. G., Sawyer, A. T., Ashley, A. W., & Oh, D. (2010). The effect of mindfulness-based therapy on anxiety and depression: A meta-analytic review. *Journal of Consulting and Clinical Psychology, 78,* 169–183. doi:10.1037/a0018555

[3]Grossman, P., Niemann, L., Schmidt, S., & Walach, H. (2004). Mindfulness-based stress reduction and health benefits: A meta-analysis. *Journal of Psychosomatic Research, 57,* 35–43. doi:10.1016/S0022-3999(03)00573-7

[4]Helpguide.org. (n.d.). *Benefits of mindfulness: Practices for improving mental and physical well-being.* Retrieved from http://www.helpguide.org/harvard/mindfulness.htm

THE FOUNDATION OF MINDFULNESS

There are a number of core features associated with mindfulness; these features vary depending on the viewpoint of the author, practitioner, or researcher.[5,6] There are however, several key foundational concepts you should be aware of. These are

- awareness,
- present focus,
- being nonjudgmental,
- beginner's mind,
- inaction, and
- observing.

Awareness

If you're like most people, your controls are set to autopilot. Throughout the day, you wander from one appointment to the next, hop from chore to chore, and have conversations you won't remember 2 hours later. But don't feel bad: As I mentioned earlier, multitasking has become a necessary art form in our culture. Engaging your autopilot is how you manage it. The problem is that you don't know when to shut it off, or if you do know, you choose to leave the autopilot on because it prevents distraction and enhances your productivity.

Focusing your awareness on one thing at a time is crucial when using mindfulness. In addition to knowing what's going on inside your mind and how you are feeling (both emotionally and physically), it's important to be aware of the things going on around you,

---

[5]Brantley, J., & Millstine, W. (2008). *Daily meditations for calming your anxious mind.* Oakland, CA: New Harbinger.
[6]Roemer, L., & Orsillo, S. M. (2008). *Mindfulness and acceptance-based behavioral therapies in practice.* New York, NY: Guilford Press.

just not all at once. Although you will be able to practice awareness in exercises later, try out the one below to get started. First, try it at a time when you are not feeling anxious at all. If you are comfortable with the process, you will eventually be able to draw on this and other mindfulness practices during times of moderate to high anxiety.

Awareness Exercise

1. Close your eyes and keep them closed for 30 seconds. Breathe slowly and deeply, feeling your abdomen rise and fall with each breath. Allow any random thoughts that pop into your head to pass through your mind like clouds passing overhead.
2. Open your eyes. Notice all the things surrounding you. See the people, furniture, computer, color of the walls, and anything else that catches your eye. Notice the temperature of the room. Hear the sounds coming from behind you.
3. Close your eyes again for 30 seconds. Continue to breathe and allow random thoughts to pass through your mind. While your eyes are closed, decide on an object to focus on exclusively when you open them.
4. Open your eyes. Focus intently on the object for 2 minutes. Look at nothing else other than the object you chose to focus on. Don't think about it. Don't label it. Don't analyze it. Just focus on it. If your eyes wander, gently and slowly bring them back to the object.

Present Focus

You may think you spend most of your day in the here and now. The reality is that you don't. Most of your day is spent shifting your thoughts back and forth between the future and the past. For example, thoughts such as "I need to get to the meeting," "What am I going to cook for dinner?" "Will the teacher like my paper?" or "What should I write in my next e-mail?" are all future-oriented, not present-oriented, thoughts. Similarly, thoughts such as "Did I forget anything during the meeting?" "Did my child finish her homework?" or "Did I turn off the stove before I left" are focused on the past and not the present. We all fill our days with this thought ping-pong. And, what do we call past- and future-oriented thoughts? You got it: *ruminations* (past) and *worry* (future), the DNA of anxiety. Therefore, learning to stay focused on the present while diverting your attention away from the past and future is key to managing your anxiety.

Being Nonjudgmental

There's quite a bit of truth to the saying that you are your own worst enemy. You drive yourself crazy trying to understand, label, and solve everything. Don't feel bad—everyone does it. It's your natural attempt to try and organize and control those things around you. It's a way for you to try to understand the world and make sense of those things that you don't understand. Considering you live in a chaotic and unpredictable world, it's pretty adaptive, at least most of the time. But again, you really beat yourself up by judging things to be good or bad and right or wrong. You create unneeded anxiety by trying to control those things that can't be controlled. And you set unrealistic and unattainable expectations for yourself that no one could live up to.

It's important to avoid judgment about who you are, what you do, other people, and everything else around you. Just accept your experiences for what they are: nothing more, nothing less. Without labels and judgments, you can't have anxiety. Labeling an upcoming first date with someone you just met as "scary" will make you anxious. Simply acknowledging that you have an upcoming date with someone you just met is void of any emotion.

Beginner's Mind

Related to the art and practice of being nonjudgmental, *beginner's mind* involves embracing life with openness, optimism, and genuine interest in new experiences while avoiding preconceived notions and labels. It asks you to set aside all of your clever, insightful, and even brilliant ideas and observations for a time. Just like taking a course in school on a subject you know nothing about, beginner's mind challenges you to look at every life experience from a beginner's perspective. In essence, judgment stifles emotional growth and feeds anxiety. Approaching life with an informed naivete is intellectually enlightening and emotionally freeing. For an example of someone who is good at the practice of beginner's mind, take a look at a newborn or infant. His or her day is filled with new experiences that generate openness and interest.

> Beginner's mind involves embracing life with openness, optimism, and genuine interest in new experiences.

Inaction

Not to be confused with laziness or apathy, *inaction*, as related to mindfulness, is the intentional refraining from doing anything. In other words, it focuses on resisting the urge to act when you are upset. It helps you avoid being impulsive, argumentative, judgmental, and the many other things you are when your emotions get the best of you. Inaction takes a lot of practice and doesn't come naturally for most of us. The next time you feel yourself getting anxious or upset, envision the urge to act as a brick wall and your desire to resist acting as a large beam holding it steady in place.

Observing

Observing is different from seeing. *Seeing* is what you do when you scan a room as you walk into it or when you watch a ball game on television. *Observing* is the process of noticing the many fine details of an object. It's describing with precise and creative detail the shape, color, size, texture, taste, smell, and various other aspects of what's being observed. Observing can also be done with abstract objects such as feelings (worry, fear, sadness).

Observing Exercise

1. Close your eyes and keep them closed for 30 seconds. Breathe slowly and deeply. Allow any random thoughts to flow effortlessly in and out of your mind.
2. While your eyes are closed, decide on an object in the room that you want to observe. Open your eyes.
3. While focusing on the object, conjure up as many adjectives as you can about the object. If your eyes wander, bring them back to the object. What do you notice? Is the object round or flat? Is it shiny or dull? Does it appear heavy or light? Is it slick, rough, fuzzy, or jagged? Is it hollow or solid? Describe the object in as much detail as possible. Pretend you are describing it to someone who has never seen it before.

BUILDING A PRACTICE OF MINDFULNESS

Now that you have an understanding of how mindfulness works, following are several techniques you can use to develop your mindfulness skills. Each exercise helps you integrate the core features of mindfulness that I listed previously. In the beginning, it's best if you stick to just one of the techniques each day. This way you can become proficient at using it. After you've mastered a technique, move on to the next one. Most likely, you'll find some techniques more useful than others. But, the more tools you can add to your toolbox, the better off you'll be. Don't become discouraged if you don't seem to "get it" in the beginning. Unless you are used to practicing these techniques on a regular basis, many will seem foreign. At first, your mind will wander, and you will be easily distracted by people and things in your environment. You may question the usefulness of these exercises as your frustration builds. Just don't give up too soon. As with every other exercise described in this book, practice is the key to success. Variations on these techniques and more can be found elsewhere.[7,8]

Awareness of Breathing Exercise

1. Allow yourself to settle into a comfortable sitting position, either on a chair or couch that supports your neck and back or on a soft surface on the floor, with your buttocks supported by cushions. Whether you use a chair or sit on the floor, make sure your spine and neck are straight. This an important point as most people tend to slump or hunch over when sitting.
2. Once you have reached an upright and comfortable posture, if sitting in a chair, place your feet flat on the floor, with your

[7]Segal, Z. V., Williams, J. G., & Teasdale, J. D. (2013). *Mindfulness-based cognitive therapy for depression* (2nd ed.). New York, NY: Guilford Press.
[8]Kabat-Zinn, J. (2005). *Full catastrophe living: Using the wisdom of your body and mind to face stress, pain, and illness* (15th anniversary ed.). New York, NY: Delta Trade Paperback/Bantam Dell.

legs uncrossed. Gently close your eyes. It may help to imagine a light thread attached to the back of your scalp pulling your head gently upwards and allowing your spine to lengthen.

3. Bring your awareness to your physical sensations by focusing your attention on the sensations of touch and pressure in your body where it makes contact with the floor and whatever you are sitting on. Spend a minute or two exploring these sensations.

4. Now bring awareness to the various physical sensations in your lower abdomen as the breath moves in and out of your body. (When you first try this practice, it may be helpful to place your hand on your lower abdomen and become aware of the changing pattern of sensations where your hand makes contact with your abdomen.)

5. Focus your awareness on the sensations of slight stretching as your stomach rises with each breath you take in, and of gentle deflation as it falls with each exhalation. As best you can, follow with your awareness the changing physical sensations in the lower abdomen all the way through as the breath enters and leaves your body. There is no need to try to control the breathing in any way—simply let the breath breathe itself.

6. As best you can, also bring this attitude of acceptance to the rest of your experience. There is nothing to be fixed, no particular state to be achieved. As best you can, simply allow your experience to be your experience, without needing it to be other than it is.

7. Do not worry when your mind wanders from the focus on the breath in the lower abdomen. This is perfectly OK—it's simply what minds do. Acknowledge this shift and gently shift your awareness back to the changing pattern of physical sensations in the lower abdomen. You may have to do this several times, especially when you first start practicing.

8. As best you can, bring a quality of kindliness to your awareness, perhaps seeing the repeated wanderings of the mind as opportunities to bring patience and gentle curiosity to your experience.

9. Continue with the practice for 15 minutes, or longer if you wish.[9]

Mindfulness of Sound Exercise

1. Find a comfortable position either lying down or sitting upright. Make sure that your spine is straight, shoulders relaxed, and jaw unclenched. Scan your body for any areas of tension and relax them if found. Make sure that you are in a place where you won't be interrupted or easily distracted.

2. Close your eyes. Using the breathing technique described above, breathe deeply until you have reached a heightened sense of relaxation and focus. Notice how your abdomen rises and falls with each soothing inhalation and exhalation. Feel the warmth of each breath as it washes through your entire body. (If you feel you need more guidance on deep breathing, put this exercise on hold and review Chapter 6.)

3. Shift awareness from your breathing and focus it on your ears. Imagine your ears becoming larger and able to catch every sound that comes in your direction. Imagine sounds from all directions spiraling, spinning, and floating toward the sides of your head.

---

[9]From *Everyday Mindfulness: A Guide to Using Mindfulness to Improve Your Well-Being and Reduce Stress and Anxiety in Your Life* (p. 12), by C. Thompson. Available at http://www.stillmind.com.au/Documents/Everyday%20Mindfulness.pdf. Adapted with permission of the author.

4. Allow the sounds to find you. Don't search for them. Experience them in their purest form. Don't label them or judge them in any way. They are not loud, soft, annoying, or pleasant. They are just sounds. Just be open to experiencing them as they happen. If you do find yourself labeling or judging them, acknowledge that you are doing so and gently redirect your focus to the sounds.

5. As your mind wanders and you become distracted by your thoughts, simply acknowledge that this has happened without being critical or becoming frustrated. You have done nothing wrong.

6. Slowly begin to filter the sounds entering your ears. Refocus your attention on your breathing. Open your eyes when ready.

Mindfulness of Thoughts Exercise

1. Find a comfortable position either lying down or sitting upright. Make sure that your spine is straight, shoulders are relaxed, and jaw is unclenched. Make sure that you are in a place where you won't be interrupted.

2. Close your eyes. Using breathing techniques you've already learned, breathe deeply until you have reached a heightened sense of relaxation and focus. Notice how your abdomen rises and falls with each soothing inhalation and exhalation. Feel the warmth of each breath as it washes through your entire body.

3. Shift awareness away from your breathing and focus it on your thoughts. As you imagine your thoughts taking a unique shape and form, experience them floating through the air en route to your mind. As they enter your mind, allow them to pass freely. Do not interrupt them or impede their flow in

any way. Avoid labeling, judging, or analyzing them. Just let them be.

4. Stay in the present. As you find yourself immersed in ruminative thoughts about the past or worrisome thoughts about the future, acknowledge that you are doing so. Refocus your attention on the shape and form of the thoughts as they enter and leave your mind. Remember, they are just thoughts—nothing more, nothing less.

5. Slowly begin to filter the thoughts entering your mind. Refocus your attention on your breathing. Open your eyes when you're ready.

Mindful Eating Exercise

1. Find a quiet and comfortable place where you can eat. Practicing mindful eating with others at the dinner table is difficult as that setting presents many distractions. You may want to find a remote space in your home, at work, or in a restaurant.

2. Pay attention to the food in front of you. Observe what it looks like. Does it appear hot or cold? What color is it? Is it in a wrapper, on a plate, or in a bowl? Observe its smell. Does it smell fresh, stale, or burnt? Does the food make your mouth water?

3. Take a bite. Notice how it tastes in your mouth. Is it salty, sweet, or both? Is the texture tough, grainy, or soft? Is it hard to chew or does it melt in your mouth? Notice how the flavor erupts in your mouth with full force and then diminishes. Feel your jaw move as you chew. Notice how your teeth tear into every morsel. Feel the chewed food slide down your throat and into your stomach.

4. Do the same thing with each bite until you're finished. Pay attention to how your stomach feels. Does it feel full or empty?

Notice the flavor that remains in your mouth. Are there bits of food stuck between your teeth? Are you thirsty?[10,11]

Mindfulness of Beauty

1. Close your eyes. Using the breathing techniques you've already learned, breathe deeply until you have reached a heightened sense of relaxation and focus. Notice how your abdomen rises and falls with each soothing inhalation and exhalation. Feel the warmth of each breath as it washes through your entire body.

2. Once you feel relaxed, close your eyes and conjure up something in your mind that you think is beautiful. It could be the face of your spouse, child, or parent. It can be a special place, a flower or painting, or blue sky filled with billowy white clouds. It can be anything that you consider beautiful.

3. Once you have the person, place, or thing in your mind, focus on what makes it beautiful for you. Is it the complexion, color, or hue? Is it the shape, texture, or smell? Is it beautiful purely because of the warm and loving emotions you associate with it? Do this for 10 minutes.

4. Once you are finished, slowly open your eyes. Immediately share your experience with someone. Describe to them this person, place, or thing you just finished observing and why it is beautiful to you. It can be with a loved one near you or over the phone. Or, if you prefer, describe its beauty through writing. Be as detailed as possible. Notice the positive emotions that fill you when you talk or write about it.

---

[10]Nhat Hanh, T., & Cheung, L. (2010). *Savor: Mindful eating, mindful life.* New York, NY: HarperCollins.
[11]Bays, J. C. (2009). *Mindful eating: A guide to rediscovering a healthy and joyful relationship with food.* Boston, MA: Shambhala.

A New Experience

1. Close your eyes. Using breathing techniques you've already learned, breathe deeply until you have reached a heightened sense of relaxation and focus. Notice how your abdomen rises and falls with each soothing inhalation and exhalation. Feel the warmth of each breath as it washes through your entire body.

2. Once you feel relaxed, look around the room and pick one object to focus on. It could be a picture, chair, bottle—anything in plain sight. Bring the object close to you or move close to the object. You want to be close enough so that you can see all of its details.

3. Look intently at the object. Imagine yourself being from a thousand years in the future. Your surroundings, including this object, are completely foreign to you. You've never seen anything like it. Be curious and open to observation and learning.

4. Observe every aspect of the object for 10 minutes. What color is it? Is it tall, short, round, or flat? What is its texture? Imagine yourself collecting as many details about the object so you can describe it to your friends when you return to where you came from.

5. After you are done observing the object, close your eyes and picture it in your mind. Conjure up all the vivid details. View it from above, below, and the side. Imagine what it looks like from the inside. Once you are finished, slowly open your eyes.

SUMMARY

You miss many of life's small wonders as a result of trying to keep up with the hectic schedule of day-to-day life. Mindfulness allows you to slow life down and savor those wonders. But you have to be open and willing to slow down and approach life from a different perspective. Here are a few points to take away from this chapter.

- Multitasking is useful in today's society, but you need to slow down and smell the roses.
- Mindfulness is focused on the present, not the past or future.
- Research is clear that mindfulness improves psychological and physical health.
- Anxiety cannot exist when you are completely focused on the present.
- Effective use of mindfulness requires practice and patience.

CHAPTER 4

ROUTINES AND HABITS AREN'T THAT IMPORTANT, ARE THEY?

To keep the body in good health is a duty . . . otherwise we shall not be able to keep our mind strong and clear.
— Hindu Prince Gautama Siddharta,
the founder of Buddhism

If you're like most people, you pay more attention to the maintenance of your car than your body. This is unfortunate, because your body is a more sensitive and complicated system than anything on the road today. Without proper upkeep, you can surely expect premature wear and tear, unusual sounds, and sluggishness going up hills (yes, I'm talking about your body). You can also expect anxiety.

It's understandable why we tend to focus our attention more on our vehicles as opposed to our bodies. Think about it. No one requires that you get a yearly physical checkup, but states require smog, safety, and other vehicle operation inspections before you can register or renew the registration on your car. You can get a ticket for emitting too much exhaust, a cracked windshield, nonworking taillights, and dangerously worn tires. Your doctor usually lets you off with a stern warning. Face it: Culturally, when it comes to habits and our health, it's live and let live.

The problem is that anxiety flourishes in a poorly maintained and unbalanced system. Lack of sleep, poor dietary habits, excessive use of caffeine and alcohol, and lack of exercise (covered in the next chapter) are the most common culprits of system neglect. If left unchecked for too long, poor lifestyle habits lead to increased emotional and physical strain. In turn, this increases worry, stress, feelings of being overwhelmed, fear, panic, and numerous other anxiety-related symptoms and problems. Overall satisfaction with life drops, health problems start to occur, and in some cases, depression sets in.

The good news is that with a plan, some effort, and a willingness to tolerate some mild discomfort, you can manage your anxiety and associated problems. This will require you to make some relatively minor adjustments to your daily schedule. Please note that I said *minor* and not *easy*. Like most things in life worth having or doing, sacrifice and hard work are required. For the techniques in this chapter to work, you need to make a commitment to yourself; you also need to make a commitment to those people in your life you care about. Never underestimate the power of promising the ones you love that you'll change. It's a great source of motivation and perseverance. Once you've made your commitments, all you need to do is follow through. Only then will you see the incredible benefits these behaviors provide in reducing anxiety to manageable levels.

> Make a commitment to yourself and to those you care about.

SLEEP

Sleep is an activity that is often taken for granted. If you have a looming deadline or if you're in the mood for some late night television, sleep is the first to suffer. If you have a lot on your mind and feel compelled to worry about it, your nightly obligation to the Sandman is cut. The fact of the matter is that getting adequate sleep is the best defense against illness, both physical and psychological.

The average adult needs between 7 and 9 hours of sleep. There are a few rare individuals who need as few as 5 and some who need as many as 10. It's important to keep in mind, however, that quantity is only one aspect of sleep; the quality of sleep is just as important, if not more so. You can sleep all day, but if your sleep is not refreshing, then you will feel tired and run down throughout the day.

> Quantity is only one aspect of sleep; the quality of sleep is just as important.

The most common cause of nonrefreshing sleep is frequent awakenings during the night. Frequent awakenings can be caused by a number of behavioral and psychological factors, including poor sleep habits, worry, and stress. Here are some tips you can use to sleep better. You can also find a number of free or low-cost smartphone apps to help you sleep, such as Sleep Pillow Sounds[1] and Sleep Tips.[2]

Sleep Tips

DEAL WITH STRESS LEFT OVER FROM EARLIER IN THE DAY. Write down your thoughts and feelings about what's been bothering you. Talk with a friend or loved one about your problems. Do something to set your mind at ease so you can be rested for whatever happens tomorrow. If you don't do something, you will pay a steep price. Leftover stress and worries from the day can wreak havoc on your ability to fall and stay asleep.

STOP THINKING ABOUT THINGS WHEN YOU ARE IN BED. As mentioned in Chapter 2, you can consolidate your daily worries into a designated worry time. Just make sure that your worry time is at least 1 hour before bedtime. Typically, 20 to 30 minutes will do the trick. One of

---

[1]Clear Sky Apps. (2013). Sleep Pillow Sounds (Version 6.4) [Mobile application software]. Retrieved from http://www.clearskyapps.com/portfolio/sleep
[2]TapCoder. (2013). Sleep Tips (Version 3.17) [Mobile application software]. Retrieved from http://www.tapcoder.com/

> The bed should be used only for sleep and sex.

two things will happen. You will either reach some decision about your situation, or you will realize how ridiculous it is to lose sleep over the problem and postpone thinking about it until tomorrow. If you must think about something while you're in bed, think about a place you'd like to go on vacation. Think about something relaxing you have done in the past and relive it in your mind. Make a conscious effort not to think about the distressing thoughts that keep playing over and over in your head.

USE THE BED FOR ONLY TWO THINGS: SLEEP AND SEX. Whenever you do things other than sleep in bed, such as watching television, reading, or playing video games, you are associating the bed with something other than sleep. So, when you get into bed because you want to go to sleep, your body and mind are gearing up to spend the next few hours watching television. Why? Because this is what you've taught them that the bed is for. Using the bed only for sleep retrains your mind and body. If you are not able to fall asleep within 15 to 20 minutes, get up and do something else for a while. But, don't do anything too interesting— fold the laundry or start a chapter in a textbook. (Who knows? Maybe this book would be good for that.) And yes, I mentioned sex. Granted, based on my logic, you can argue that having sex in bed associates the bed with sex, leading to the same problems caused by television, reading, and playing video games. That may be true . . . in theory. But, sex is a great way to reduce stress and anxiety. It facilitates a neurochemical cascade that will put the most wired person to sleep. Plus, in all my years of practicing psychology, I've never had a patient complain to me that his or her sex life was interfering with sleep.

USE THE HOUR OR TWO BEFORE BED AS A TIME TO LET YOUR MIND AND BODY CALM DOWN. An hour or two before bedtime is not the time to run sprints on the treadmill, eat a big spicy burrito, or get into an argument with your spouse. Prepare yourself for sleep. Pre-bed routines can be helpful. Read the kids a bedtime story, take a hot shower, or make lunch for the next day. Go for a brief but slow walk. Just do the same thing each night so that your body and brain know what's coming next.

SET A SPECIFIC TIME TO WAKE UP AND GO TO SLEEP. The more your wake-and-rise schedule is fixed, the better your body and mind will respond when you want to fall asleep and when you want to get up. As I mentioned above, the mind and body love routines. However, if you find yourself saying, "Easy enough, I'll just sleep in on the weekends," then I have to burst your bubble: Your sleep and wake schedule should carry over to the weekends as well. Trying to catch up on your sleep over the weekend does nothing more than get you off schedule for Monday, which leads to a week-long struggle to regain balance. To break this vicious cycle, get up and go to bed the same time on Saturday and Sunday that you do on Monday and Tuesday.

DON'T NAP TOO LATE IN THE DAY. Historically, experts have advised not napping at all. However, research shows that a short catnap can reduce fatigue and increase energy and focus during the day. The key is to keep it short (15 minutes) and take this truncated snooze in the early to mid-afternoon. Don't take a nap when you get home from work or after dinner, which will make getting to bed later difficult.

Not sure how to make these sleep tips work for you? Maybe Sandra's story will help you see how one person incorporated minor—though not necessarily easy—changes into her routine, with good results.

Sandra, a high school teacher and mother of two toddlers, complained to her doctor that she was having problems sleeping. Her doctor referred her to a psychologist for help. During the psychologist's interview with Sandra, it became apparent that she was engaging in a number of maladaptive behaviors that were contributing to her sleep problems. Not only was Sandra spending 1 to 2 hours every night lying in bed worrying about work, she was also grading papers and watching television.

Realizing that she was having trouble sleeping, she began going to the gym after putting the kids to bed. She had heard that exercise was a great way to improve sleep. Because she was so tired and run down after getting the kids to bed, on the way to the gym each day she'd stop by the gas station and buy an energy drink. This gave her the boost she needed to get through the workout.

The psychologist pointed out to Sandra how many of her evening routines were responsible for her sleep problems. He recommended that she find a way to exercise earlier in the day. He asked her to schedule 20 minutes each evening when she could worry about all the things going on at work. He also recommended to Sandra that on nights when she found it necessary to work from home, she do it at the kitchen table and not in the bed. He stressed to her the importance of associating the bed only with sleep.

Sandra made the minor adjustments to her schedule. She decided to stop off at the gym on her way home from work. She replaced the energy drink with a bottle of water and protein bar. Every night from 7:00 to 7:20, she did nothing but worry about work. After only a few days of prescribed worrying, she found that she no longer needed to do it. And on the nights when she needed to grade papers, she did it at the dining room table while her husband gave the kids a bath. Within a week, Sandra was sleeping soundly.

Nightmares

Nightmares are a common cause of sleep disturbances, leading to increased stress and anxiety during the day. In fact, nightmares are a common symptom of posttraumatic stress disorder, which is an anxiety disorder that develops after a traumatic event. Trauma is not the only cause of nightmares, however. Virtually every human will have a nightmare at least once in his or her lifetime. In fact, some studies have shown that up to 25% of people have a nightmare at least once a month. Here are a few tips for managing these nighttime spoilers.

REMIND YOURSELF THAT BAD DREAMS ARE NORMAL AND COMMON. Whether it's after a traumatic event or not, nightmares are common and expected. Experiencing a nightmare (or several) doesn't mean you are crazy. It just means you are human.

THINK OF PLEASANT AND POSITIVE EVENTS PRIOR TO SLEEP. What we think about right before sleep is connected to what we dream about. Using a computer programming analogy, Garbage In During Wakefulness = Garbage Out During Sleep. Don't spend the time leading up to bed thinking about distressing things. Also, don't watch scary movies, read graphic thrillers, or play violent video games right before bed. The images can follow you into sleep. Instead, think about past positive experiences like your last vacation, watching your child take his or her first steps, or going to a carnival with your parents when you were a child. You're better off having memories of sandy beaches and cotton candy follow you into your dreams.

> Garbage In During Wakefulness = Garbage Out During Sleep

OVERCOME THE FEAR OF GOING BACK TO SLEEP. Many who experience nightmares on a frequent basis report fears about going back to sleep after being awakened by a nightmare. Nightmares are thoughts during your sleep. And just like thoughts, they cannot hurt you. Remind yourself of this next time you're fearful of falling back to sleep. The same advice you give to your children about nightmares applies to you as well. If you find that you are too emotional to drift back to sleep, spend a few minutes in bed focusing on positive and calming thoughts. Just long enough to get your heart rate and blood pressure back down.

KEEP A NIGHTMARE JOURNAL. Documenting how often, what type, and how disturbing your nightmares are can help you gain a sense of mastery over them. It can also help you determine whether there is a theme to your dreams and monitor whether they are getting worse, better, or staying the same. This technique is very helpful if you are already seeing a therapist, as you can bring your journal to session and talk about the specifics of your dreams. You can keep a journal by your bed, or if you are a fan of smartphone apps, you can use Dream Tracker,[3] which allows you to keep track of your dreams and associated emotions on your phone.

CHANGE THE DREAM. Research has shown that changing the disturbing content of a dream to something more pleasant or neutral reduces the frequency and intensity of nightmares.[4] Choose a dream you'd like to change, decide how you would like to change it, and visually rehearse the new, less disturbing dream twice a day for 15 to 20 minutes. If this becomes too difficult, however, you may want to consult with a mental health professional to assist you. You can find information about seeking out professional help in Chapter 10.

---

[3]Perpetuum Media. (2012). Dream Tracker (Version 1.3) [Mobile application software]. Retrieved from https://itunes.apple.com/us/app/dream-tracker/id533368370?mt=8

[4]Krakow, B. (2002). *Turning nightmares into dreams*. Albuquerque, NM: Maimonides Sleep Arts and Sciences.

CAFFEINE

Moderation is the key for most people when it comes to caffeine. A little bit here and there is harmless. However, for people with anxiety, even small amounts can be problematic. For example, people who experience significant anxiety, panic symptoms in particular (racing heart, feeling of impending doom, sweating), are more sensitive to the effects of caffeine. Caffeine can actually induce a full-blown panic attack, which is a combination of highly distressing psychological and physical fear-based symptoms (see the following chart for symptoms of a panic attack). At a minimum, caffeine mimics many of the symptoms associated with panic.[5] This can lead to increased worry and risk of actually having an attack. Short of panic, caffeine also causes jitteriness, trembling, and feelings of nervousness and apprehension. It also fuels worry, restlessness, and irritability.

> Caffeine mimics many of the symptoms associated with panic.

What Is Caffeine?

Caffeine stimulates both the brain and body and is the most widely used mind-altering drug in the world. It is used primarily as a means of restoring alertness and focus by blocking the chemical adenosine, which is responsible for promoting sleep. Caffeine is both a natural and synthetic (human-made) chemical found in a variety of beverages, such as coffee, soda, tea, and the ever-popular energy drinks. It is also found in certain foods (chocolate) and some medicines (headache pain relievers).

---

[5]American Psychiatric Association. (2000). *Diagnostic and statistical manual of mental Disorders* (4th ed., text rev.). Washington, DC: Author.

Symptoms of a Panic Attack Compared With the Effects of Caffeine	
Symptoms of a panic attack	Effects of caffeine
• Racing heart • Sweating • Difficulty breathing • Discomfort in the chest and stomach • Dizziness • Feeling disconnected from reality • Sense of losing control or dying • Shakiness, trembling, or tingling in extremities	• Racing heart • Stomach discomfort • Lightheadedness • Feeling hot or flushed • Shakiness and trembling • Anxiety/nervousness • Difficulty falling asleep • Feeling disconnected from reality

How Much Is Too Much?

In moderate doses (200–300 milligrams or two to four cups of coffee daily), caffeine is considered safe and causes no noticeable problems in the average person. However, people with anxiety cannot tolerate as much caffeine as those without anxiety and should be careful when getting their morning or afternoon fix. It is also important to be aware of the caffeine level of your favorite drink, food, or medicine. Levels vary considerably. What may seem like a small cup of Joe or a harmless piece of candy can cause your anxiety to skyrocket. Following are caffeine levels of some commonly consumed beverages, foods, and medicines.[6,7]

---

[6]Caffeine Informer. (n.d.). *Caffeine informer*. Retrieved from http://www.caffeineinformer.com

[7]University of Michigan, University Health Service. (n.d.). *Caffeine*. Retrieved from http://www.uhs.umich.edu/caffeine

Caffeine Levels in Common Foods, Beverages, and Medicines

Chocolate	Average
Chocolate milk (8 oz.)	8 mg
Milk chocolate (1 oz.)	7 mg
Semi-sweet chocolate (1 oz.)	18 mg
Unsweetened chocolate (1 oz.)	25 mg
Coffee	
Brewed (6 oz.)	100 mg
Instant (1 rounded tsp)	57 mg
Brewed decaffeinated (6 oz.)	3 mg
Instant decaffeinated (1 rounded tsp)	2 mg
Cappuccino (4 oz.)	100 mg
Espresso (2 oz.)	100 mg
Latte (single)	50 mg
Other beverages (12 oz.)	
Coca-Cola, Diet Coke	46 mg
Dr. Pepper, Diet Dr. Pepper	40 mg
Mountain Dew	54 mg
Pepsi-Cola, Diet Pepsi	38 mg
Red Bull (8.2 oz.)	80 mg
5-hour ENERGY	138 mg
Monster Energy	160 mg
Tea (5 oz.)	
Brewed, green or black, U.S. brands (3 min.)	40 mg
Brewed, imported brands	60 mg
Instant (1 tsp)	30 mg
Iced (8 oz.)	25 mg
Decaffeinated	5 mg

(continues)

99

Caffeine Levels in Common Foods, Beverages, and Medicines *(Continued)*	
Nonprescription drugs	**Average**
Caffeine tablets	
NoDoz	100 mg
Vivarin	200 mg
Pain relievers (per tablet)	
Anacin	32 mg
Excedrin	65 mg
Midol (maximum strength)	60 mg

Note. Retrieved from University Health Service, University of Michigan, at http://www.uhs.umich.edu/caffeine.

Should I Quit?

If you experience increased anxiety after using caffeine, then the simple answer is: Yes! But this is a personal decision, just like losing weight or quitting smoking. Letting go of caffeine is not easy, especially if you've been drinking large amounts of it for many years. But if you are one of those people who are more sensitive to caffeine, then it's time to stop. Following is a detailed plan for helping you be successful.

Six Steps to Cutting Caffeine From Your Day

1. Identify why quitting is important to you. Write down at least three reasons. One obvious reason is to help you better manage your anxiety. However, there are many other benefits to quitting, such as reducing high blood pressure, improving sleep, and saving money. Keep these reasons with you at all times. You can jot them down on a 3 × 5 index card, business

card, or even a restaurant napkin—it doesn't really matter. The important thing is to keep them with you so you can pull them out and remind yourself of them while you're standing outside of Starbucks or about to order a large glass of iced tea at your favorite restaurant.

2. Educate yourself about withdrawal symptoms. Yes, you can have withdrawal symptoms from caffeine. Fortunately, they tend to be mild in most people and only reach the level of being a nuisance. The most typical withdrawal effects are
   - headache,
   - fatigue,
   - sleepiness/drowsiness,
   - insomnia,
   - concentration problems,
   - irritability/agitation, and
   - flu-like symptoms.

3. Choose a start date. This may seem like a no-brainer, but you'd be surprised how many people never put a plan into action because they haven't decided on when to start. Choose a start date that is realistic. It may be next week or next month. If the next couple of weeks are going to be unusually stressful, then start after things settle down. And don't try to quit too many things at one time. If you are already trying to quit smoking, cutting back on carbs, or kicking gluten out of your dietary routine, conquer those things first. The worst thing you can do is set yourself up for failure by trying to make radical changes in your routine.

   > Choose a start date that is realistic.

4. Track your caffeine intake. You will need to track how much caffeine you take in each day. You can make up a simple chart or download one of the several caffeine trackers available

for smart phones (Coffee Addict[8] or Caffeine Monitor[9]). Estimate your daily caffeine intake over a period of 1 week. Once you know how much caffeine you take in, you can proceed to Step 5.

5. Cut back gradually. Avoid quitting cold turkey. Reducing your caffeine intake gradually helps prevent withdrawal symptoms. A general rule of thumb is to reduce your intake by 50% each week. So, if you normally drink eight cups (600–800 milligrams of caffeine) of coffee a day, you would cut back to four cups a day the first week, two cups the second week, one cup the third week, and one-half cup or stop altogether the fourth week.

6. Increase your fluid intake. As you reduce liquid, even if it's coffee or soda, it's important to replace it with noncaffeinated beverages to avoid dehydration and headaches. An ideal replacement is water, which helps the kidneys flush toxins out of your system. It also keeps you hydrated. If you need to add a little flavor to your life, try drinking a reduced calorie, noncaffeinated sports drink or flavored vitamin water.

ALCOHOL

Second only to exercise, alcohol is the oldest method for the self-management of anxiety. And it is the most common form in use today, surpassing meditation, psychotherapy, and prescription medication combined. Why is it so common? The short answer is that it works. Yes, alcohol is a very effective means for reducing uncomfortable anxiety in the short term. You know this if you've had a drink or

---

[8]NetDev. (2013). Coffee Addict (Version 2.0) [Mobile application software]. Retrieved from http://www.coffeeaddictapp.com/
[9]biolithic. (2013). Caffeine Monitor (Version 1.5) [Mobile application software]. Retrieved from http://biolithic.tumblr.com/

two after a tough day of work, or after a fight with a loved one, or as a way to relieve nervousness associated with an important upcoming presentation. Unfortunately, the effects are short lived, and alcohol use almost always ultimately worsens anxiety.

Why Alcohol Does and Does Not Work

Alcohol is a central nervous system depressant. In other words, it reduces activity in the brain. Alcohol slows thinking, the ability to process information, and reaction time. This is why it's so critical that you never drink and drive.

Alcohol increases the levels of the neurotransmitter in the brain called gamma-aminobutyric acid, or GABA, which is responsible for keeping people calm and relaxed and for promoting a sense of well-being. If people have too much, though, they start to lose inhibitions and become sluggish and sedated. These same effects are also seen with the class of drugs called benzodiazepines (Xanax, Valium), which are commonly prescribed for anxiety.

Although alcohol works rapidly and is effective for immediate anxiety, the pleasant effects wear off quickly and the anxiety comes rushing back. And it often comes back stronger than before. The person may then begin to use alcohol more frequently and in higher quantities to experience the same pleasant effects. If left unchecked, tolerance and dependence can develop, leading to even more problems. Alcohol can also become a crutch. For example, people who use alcohol to overcome social anxiety (nervousness and fear in public) may avoid social situations unless they are able to drink beforehand.

Alcohol also has negative effects on sleep. Granted, a few glasses of wine can help you fall asleep faster, but your sleep stages are disrupted, and you awaken prematurely as the alcohol leaves your body. Both of these processes lead to feeling tired, irritable, and hungover the next morning—a perfect prelude to a day filled with anxiety.

Recognize and Cope

Now that you understand alcohol is a common, but unhealthy, way to deal with chronic stress and anxiety, the next steps are to learn to recognize what causes you to reach for the bottle and how to cope without it. The following exercise can help. You can find the blank version of Recognizing Causes of Consuming Alcohol Worksheet at http://pubs.apa.org/books/supp/moore.

Last, regarding your alcohol use, if you think you have a problem with alcohol, you should seek professional help. You can find more information on selecting a mental health professional in Chapter 10. The CAGE Questionnaire[10] can help you assess the presence of a problem. In general, if you answer yes to one or more of the questions, you should consult with a professional. The questions for CAGE (which is an abbreviation based on the terms in bold) are as follows:

C: Have you ever felt you should **cut** down on your drinking?
A: Have people **annoyed** you by criticizing your drinking?
G: Have you ever felt bad or **guilty** about your drinking?
E: Eye opener: Have you ever had a drink first thing in the morning to steady your nerves or to get rid of a hangover?

NUTRITION

Anxiety is not necessarily caused by what you eat, but that doesn't mean what you eat isn't contributing to your anxiety. For example, certain nutrients that you take in are involved in the production of

---

[10]Ewing, J. A. (1984). Detecting alcoholism: The CAGE questionnaire. *Journal of the American Medical Association, 252,* 1905–1907.

Recognizing Causes of Consuming Alcohol

1. Describe a time or situation in which you used alcohol to cope with your stress or anxiety. Be as detailed as possible.
   <u>Last weekend I was invited to a party where I was supposed to meet this guy for the first time. I was nervous about meeting him. I had seen him before, but he had never seen me. Before I got to the party, I drank three glasses of wine to loosen up.</u>

2. Describe how alcohol was helpful to you in this situation. Did it reduce your stress or anxiety? Did it give you more confidence?
   <u>The wine helped me overcome my anxiety enough so that I could make it to the party. I wasn't more confident. I just didn't care as much.</u>

3. How was alcohol harmful to you in this situation? Be honest with yourself.
   <u>By the time I got to the party, I was already feeling dizzy from the wine. My friend also said I was slurring my words. After having a few more drinks at the party, I ended up embarrassing myself. Although I don't remember everything, my friend said I was hanging all over the guy and talking real loudly. I haven't seen him since. Plus, I think my anxiety has gotten worse. I'm supposed to go to a party next weekend and I'm more anxious about that one than the one from two weeks ago.</u>

4. Where did you learn that using alcohol was an acceptable way to manage stress and anxiety? Did you learn it from your parents, friends, television, etc?
   <u>My mom struggled with anxiety. I remember watching her drink and take anxiety pills before going out in public and to family events during the holidays. She used to embarrass the whole family when she had too much to drink or took too many of her pills.</u>

5. List three beliefs you currently hold that caused you to believe alcohol is an effective way to deal with anxiety.
   a. <u>My mom did it for years so it must work to some degree.</u>
   b. <u>Deep breathing isn't going to help with my level of anxiety.</u>
   c. <u>Most people have a few drinks before going on a first date or to a party.</u>

(continues)

Recognizing Causes of Consuming Alcohol *(Continued)*

6. List an alternative, challenging, or counter statement to each of the beliefs in Question 5.

   a. <u>It didn't work for my mom. She embarrassed everyone and eventually stopped going out at all.</u>

   b. <u>I've never tried relaxation techniques. Maybe they would help.</u>

   c. <u>Most people don't. My friends don't. The guy at the party wasn't drinking.</u>

7. List three positive ways in which you could have dealt with this situation differently.

   a. <u>I could have practiced the relaxation exercises my friend told me about.</u>

   b. <u>I could have talked with my friend about how anxious I was. I could have also told the guy at the party how I was feeling. He may have found that to be funny.</u>

   c. <u>I could have gone to the gym before the party. Exercise always seems to relax me.</u>

8. Close your eyes and imagine yourself doing these positive behaviors. On a scale of 1 to 10 (1 = *no chance;* 10 = *definite*), rate how likely you would engage in each of the positive behaviors if faced with the same or similar situation. Explain any ratings below a rating of 7.

   a. <u>7</u> (rating):_____(explanation)

   b. <u>4</u> (rating): <u>My friend would probably joke about it, which would make me upset. I also don't want my date to think I have "issues."</u> (explanation)

   c. <u>8</u> (rating):_____(explanation)

---

neurotransmitters. Neurotransmitters play a critical role in mood, including anxiety. Diet can also influence your anxiety through chemical interactions outside of the brain. Many food additives can influence vital organs such as the liver and kidneys, which can in turn influence your anxiety level through dysregulation of a number of hormones, enzymes, and other chemicals. Therefore, it is important to be mindful of what you eat and cut back on those foods that may be contributing to your anxiety.

Sugar can be problematic for people with anxiety. When you ingest sugar, the levels of sugar in your blood spike. And as the expression "What goes up must come down" so aptly points out, a drop in blood sugar levels will occur. For most people, the change in levels is unnoticeable. For others, particularly those who are more sensitive to sugar and/or have a history of anxiety, the change can be dramatic. In fact, a dramatic drop in blood sugar, also referred to as *hypoglycemia*, mimics many of the same symptoms of anxiety (shaking, dizziness, increased heart rate). One solution is to cut back on sugar, also known as simple carbohydrates. These foods include ice cream, candy, cake, soda, fruit juice, and many others—basically, the foods you already know you should be eating in moderation. At the same time, increase your intake of complex carbohydrates. Complex carbohydrates are denser in vitamins and minerals and take longer to digest, leading to less dramatic and noticeable dips and spikes in blood sugar. This type of carbohydrate is also believed to increase levels of the neurotransmitter serotonin in the brain, which is involved in reducing anxiety among other things. Examples of complex carbs include whole grains, some fruits (oranges, plums, pears, grapefruits), vegetables, and legumes (lentils, black beans, peas, soybeans).

> A dramatic drop in blood sugar, also referred to as *hypoglycemia*, mimics many of the same symptoms of anxiety.

Salt (sodium) increases blood pressure, which in turn places increased stress on the body. This increased stress can lead to chronic problems. High blood pressure also increases heart rate, which can trigger panic attacks. However, salt is an important mineral and helps maintain a healthy system. It should not be eliminated from the diet but should be reduced if appropriate. The recommended daily allowance is 2,300 milligrams, or 1,500 milligrams if you are over 51 years of age; Black; or have high blood pressure, diabetes, or kidney disease. To put these recommended levels in perspective, the average American takes in around 3,400 milligrams of sodium a day.[11]

Making some minor adjustments to your diet can pay noticeable dividends when it comes to reducing your anxiety. Plus, it helps maintain your overall physical health and can ward off problems such as diabetes, hypertension, cancer, and heart disease. To learn more about nutrition and health, visit http://www.nutrition.gov or http://www.hsph.harvard.edu/nutritionsource/.

SUMMARY

How you treat your body has a lot to do with how anxious you are. The lifestyle changes I discussed before are relatively easy to implement, but they will require some work and sacrifice on your part. If you do put in the work and effort, you will most certainly experience a reduction in your anxiety. Here are a few points to take away from this chapter.

- A poorly maintained body is a breeding ground for anxiety.
- The effects of caffeine mimic symptoms of anxiety and panic.
- Adequate sleep is important for preventing and reducing anxiety.
- Alcohol increases anxiety, disrupts sleep, and develops into a psychological crutch in some people.
- Certain foods can lead to increased levels of anxiety.

---

[11]U.S. Department of Agriculture and U.S. Department of Health and Human Services. (2010). *Dietary guidelines for Americans 2010*. Retrieved from http://www.health.gov/dietaryguidelines/dga2010/dietaryguidelines2010.pdf

CHAPTER 5

I FEEL ANXIOUS ABOUT EXERCISING . . . SO HOW CAN THAT HELP?

Thinking about working out burns 0 calories, 0 percentage of fat, and accomplishes 0 goals!

—Gwen Ro, fitness expert

Exercise is likely the oldest form of self-management of anxiety, although alcohol is a close second. Numerous studies have been conducted over recent years showing that exercise alone, or in combination with psychotherapy, is effective in reducing anxiety associated with a variety of anxiety disorders. In fact, one study found that a regular exercise program is as effective as medication in people with panic disorder.[1] This is good news, especially for those who are opposed to taking medication. As you will learn in Chapter 10, medications used to treat anxiety come with many risks and side effects and can negatively interact with other medications and with alcohol. Plus, many people object to taking psychiatric medications on sheer principle. In addition to being effective for panic disorder, exercise has also been shown to be useful for preventing other types of emotional distress. According to the Anxiety and Depression Association

---

[1]Smits, J. J., Tart, C. D., Rosenfield, D., & Zvolensky, M. J. (2011). The interplay between physical activity and anxiety sensitivity in fearful responding to carbon dioxide challenge. *Psychosomatic Medicine, 73,* 498–503. doi:10.1097/PSY.0b013e318229992b

of America,[2] people who engage in regular vigorous exercise are 25% less likely to develop general anxiety or depression 5 years later.

WHY DOES EXERCISE HELP?

It's not fully known why exercise is effective in ridding and preventing anxiety, but research indicates it's related to several reasons.[3,4]

It PROMOTES A SENSE OF WELL-BEING. Vigorous and sustained physical activity promotes the release of *endorphins*, neurotransmitters in the brain that promote a sense of euphoria and contentment. In essence, they are the body's own natural opiates. They are responsible for what is referred to as "runner's high" in joggers. This phenomenon allows joggers to overcome fatigue and pain during long-distance running. In some cases, exercise junkies become addicted to this natural sense of well-being and spend hours and hours each week searching for their next fix. But don't worry: You don't have to take out a second mortgage to finance a room full of treadmills to support your new lifestyle. Endorphin release can be achieved at modest levels of various types of exercise.

It KEEPS YOU WELL. There are countless physical benefits to regular exercise. Fighting off illness is certainly one of them. Exercise strengthens the immune system, which is important for preventing

---

[2]Anxiety and Depression Association of America. (n.d.). *Exercise for stress and anxiety.* Retrieved from http://www.adaa.org/living-with-anxiety/managing-anxiety/exercise-stress-and-anxiety

[3]Mayo Clinic. (2011). *Depression and anxiety: Exercise eases symptoms.* Retrieved from www.mayoclinic.com/health/depression-and-exercise/MH00043

[4]Exercise and immunity. (n.d.). In *Medline Plus.* Retrieved from www.nlm.nih.gov/medlineplus/ency/article/007165.htm

sickness. Researchers believe that exercise fights off infections by expelling bacteria from the lungs and toxins through sweat (the natural process of your body cooling itself) and urine (the more you exercise, the more you drink). During exercise, the body also increases circulation of white blood cells (disease fighters) and possibly slows the growth of bacteria, because of elevated body temperature. Exercise also slows the release of the stress hormone cortisol into the bloodstream, which is the immune system's archenemy. However, the opposite can occur when the level of exercise is too extreme: Overdoing it can actually weaken the body, increasing the chances of infection. A good rule of thumb is to start slow and build up your physical endurance, especially if you haven't exercised in a while. To start, you may want to work with a personal trainer or friend who exercises regularly, or use one of the many available smartphone apps (e.g., *Fitness Buddy*,[5] *Exercise Tracker*,[6] or *Start running!*[7]).

It Promotes Meditation and Focus. The ability to block out the countless persistent and often annoying sounds of your surroundings is a great way to fend off stress and anxiety. Meditation through exercise is one tool to help you do this. Exercise forces a person to focus on his or her breathing and movement, which are inherently rhythmic. Both induce a mild form of trance, allowing a brief, but effective, means for staying in the present and deflecting anxious thoughts. One note of caution, though: It's important to always be aware of your surroundings, especially if you are exercising outdoors. If you're

[5]Azumio. (2013). *Fitness Buddy* (Version 1.0) [Mobile application software]. Retrieved from http://www.fitnessbuddyapp.com
[6]HealtheHuman. (2010). *Exercise Tracker* (Version 1.12) [Mobile application software]. Retrieved from https://itunes.apple.com/us/app/exercise-tracker/id293603711?mt=8
[7]Red Rock Apps. (2013). *Start running!* (Version 1.2) [Mobile application software]. Retrieved from http://redrockapps.com/

The ability to block out your surroundings is a great way to fend off anxiety.

not careful, you may find yourself unintentionally ignoring traffic and other safety hazards. To get started, you may want to exercise in a more confined area such as a neighborhood or fitness center. Many gyms offer a 30-day free trial membership—don't be afraid to take them up on their offer.

It Relaxes the Body. The body has an internal sauna built right into its framework: It's called temperature. Just like spending 20 to 30 minutes in a steam room, exercise pushes people's internal mercury higher, which in turn promotes a sense of relaxation. But again, you don't want to overdo it. If you feel yourself becoming overheated (no longer sweating, feeling sick to your stomach, or getting dizzy), pull back on the intensity.

It Promotes Confidence. Setting realistic and achievable exercise goals, and then meeting those goals, is a surefire way to boost your confidence. Even accomplishing small goals such as walking 10 minutes per day after dinner pays sizeable emotional dividends.

SET GOALS AND DEVELOP AN EXERCISE PLAN

Setting realistic and achievable exercise goals is more difficult than you may think. For example, you want to push yourself hard enough by setting goals that are challenging; however, if you set goals that are too far out of reach, you risk damaging your confidence. You also risk physical injury by doing too much too soon. If either of these occur, you are more likely to give up on exercise.

It is important to consider two types of goals when developing an exercise plan: short term and long term. *Short-term goals* are those goals you want to achieve within the near future. For example, a short-term goal may be to buy a new pair of jogging shoes, join a health club, walk three times during the first week of your new exercise program, or lose 6 pounds during the first month. *Long-term goals* are more future oriented and generally require completion of previously set short-term goals. Examples include running an 8-minute mile, reaching your ideal body weight, or completing a half marathon by the end of the year.

Both types of goals should be realistic, achievable, and concrete. An example of a realistic, achievable, and concrete goal is to take a 20-minute walk 3 days per week between 6 and 7 p.m. An example of an unrealistic, unachievable, and nonconcrete goal is to run for a long distance 7 days per week before work. First off, "long distance" leaves too much to interpretation. Second, even elite athletes don't exercise every day. And if you are like most people, the urge to stay in bed before work is very strong. Once you decide on your short-term and long-term exercise goals, list them in the following manner.

> Goals should be realistic, achievable, and concrete.

Short-Term and Long-Term Exercise Goals

My short-term goals are

1. _____
   Date to accomplish by: _____
2. _____
   Date to accomplish by: _____

My long-term goals are

1. _____
   Date to accomplish by: _____
2. _____
   Date to accomplish by: _____

If you find that you need more help developing your exercise goals, you can use the SMART mnemonic, spelled out below. Originally developed for managers, SMART has become a popular method for setting goals.[8] The SMART acronym stands for

> **S:** Specific (State exactly what you want to achieve.)
> **M:** Measurable (How will you know that you've achieved your goal?)
> **A:** Attainable (Make sure you can reach your goal; is it realistic?)
> **R:** Relevant (How does it help you meet your overall purpose?)
> **T:** Time-bound (What is your target date for achieving your goal?)

Following is an example. A blank Setting SMART Goals Worksheet is included at http://pubs.apa.org/books/supp/moore.

Once you have identified and listed your short- and long-term goals and started exercising, use the following Exercise Log to keep track of your progress. The first few lines have been done for you as an example, and you can find a blank Exercise Log at http://pubs.apa.org/books/supp/moore. Or, as I mentioned before, you can use one of the many available smartphone exercise apps.

EXERCISE KILLERS!

Excuses, or what I like to call "exercise killers," are lurking in every nook and cranny of your mind. They are poised and ready to take out any thought or behavior intended to motivate you. These activity

---

[8]Doran, G. T. (1981). There's a S.M.A.R.T. way to write management's goals and objectives. *Management Review*, 70, pp. 35–36.

Setting Smart Goals Worksheet

Specific	**List the specific goal you would like to accomplish.** My goal is to exercise at least three times each week for the first month of my new exercise routine.
Measurable	**How will you know that your achieved your goal?** I will keep track of my exercise sessions on my smartphone app. At the end of 4 weeks, I should be able to count 12 sessions.
Attainable	**Is your goal realistic? Are there roadblocks that will prevent you from being successful?** My goal is realistic. Lack of motivation and work schedule are potential obstacles, but I can overcome them.
Relevant	**How does this goal help you with what you are trying to accomplish?** It helps me reach my ultimate goals of decreasing my stress, improving my mood, and becoming physically healthier.
Time-bound	**By what date do you need to reach your goal?** I will complete my goal by October 1, which is exactly 4 weeks from tomorrow.

Exercise Log

Week of _____

Day	Type of exercise	Duration	Difficulty	Notes
Monday	Walking	22 minutes	3	This seemed too easy. Need to push myself more to get the endorphin rush. I want a more immediate feeling of happiness after exercise.
Tuesday	Swimming	35 minutes	6	Found myself making excuses not to exercise, so pushed off swimming until the latest possible moment in the day, then couldn't sleep.
Wednesday	None	0	0	It's OK that I didn't exercise today. I am easing into my new routine. Packing all my gear for another swim first thing tomorrow morning so I have no reason to delay.

Exercise Log *(Continued)*

Thursday	Swimming	35 minutes	6	Felt embarrassed about my lack of swimming skill, as there was a water aerobics class in the adjoining lane at 6:30 a.m. Maybe I'll go when they aren't there. Or just quit caring that they might be judging me. Probably some of them can't even swim.
Friday	Jogging, walking	45 minutes	7	Went several times around the soccer field while kids were at practice. Very anxious that others were watching me and almost tripped on a tree root. I got tired quickly and had to walk.

Excuses are exercise killers.

assassins are plentiful, accurate, and lethal to any haphazard or poorly thought out plan. If you are going to be successful in your exercise endeavors, it's important to be aware of excuses. Below are some of the more common ones. For more on excuses people use to get out of exercising, see Chapter 5 in Edmund Bourne's *Coping With Anxiety: 10 Simple Ways to Relieve Anxiety, Fear & Worry*[9] and Scott Quill's online article *21 Ways to Overcome Exercise Excuses.*[10]

I'M TOO BUSY. Trust me. I know how busy you are. But there is more than enough time in your day to work in 20 to 30 minutes of exercise. Did you know the average American watches 34 hours of television each week? Yes, I said 34. That averages out to around 5 hours a day. If you exercise 30 minutes a day for 4 days per week, that leaves you 32 hours to sit in front of the boob tube. Not the average American? Say you only watch 10 hours a week. Cut that down to 8 and you can get your exercise in. You can also exercise during your lunch break or get up 30 minutes earlier in the morning.

IT'S SO BORING. It can be, if you do the same thing over and over. When starting a new exercise program, most people think of walking or jogging. Fortunately, there are dozens of other activities you can do to get into shape. If you find jogging boring, try the other activities listed below. Regardless of which ones you choose, the

---

[9]Bourne, E. (2003). *Coping with anxiety: 10 simple ways to relieve anxiety, fear & worry*. Oakland, CA: New Harbinger.
[10]Quill, S. (2013, July 2). 21 ways to overcome exercise excuses. *Men's Health.* Available at http://www.menshealth.com/mhlists/overcome_exercise_excuses/

important thing is to keep your exercise routine interesting. Activities besides walking or jogging include the following:

swimming	indoor rock climbing
bicycling	pilates
hiking	playing with your children
housework	tennis or racquet ball
playing frisbee or catch	sex (yes, sex is a vigorous
walking the dog	activity that increases
pushing a stroller	heart rate and reduces
dancing	stress)

If you still find exercise boring, try listening to music or watching television while you do it, or find a workout partner who will keep you motivated.

I'M AFRAID IT WILL CAUSE ME TO HAVE A PANIC ATTACK. For people who experience panic, exercise can be anxiety provoking. Exercise increases your heart rate and respiration, which are two common symptoms of panic attacks. To counter this anxiety, it's important to remind yourself that there is a very good reason why your heart is beating fast and you are breathing heavily—you're exercising! A person experiencing a true panic attack is generally unaware of the cause of the racing heart and increased breathing. Another helpful tactic is to just take it slow. Let your body and mind get used to the feelings and thoughts associated with the physiological consequences of exercise. Over time, you will become more comfortable with them.

GETTING STARTED IS EXPENSIVE. It is, if you go out and buy a $200 pair of running shoes and sign a multiyear contract at the newest health club and spa. Stay away from the mall and visit a national chain sporting goods store. You can find a suitable pair of shoes for between $30 and $50. And before you sign your life away at your neighborhood gym, start exercising outside. It's free, and the scenery is excellent.

I DON'T KNOW WHAT TO DO; PEOPLE WILL LAUGH AT ME. This excuse often keeps people from joining a gym or only going once or twice and never going back. It's understandable—the different types of exercise machines you find at your local gym look like something out of a sci-fi thriller. The truth is that they are not as complicated as you might think. Plus, most gyms will provide you a free orientation to the equipment. But if you are overly self-conscious, avoid peak times, which are between 7 and 10 in the morning and between 4 and 7 in the evening. And as far as people laughing at you, you can let go of that distorted belief now: People aren't paying attention to you. They are caught up in their own feelings of insecurity, focused on their movement and breathing, or in the case of the gym rat, too focused on themselves to care about what's going on with you.

EXERCISING WILL JUST MAKE ME EAT MORE. It will, but you burn off those extra calories, plus some. Exercise increases your hunger because it's your body's way of telling you that you need more energy to keep up with the pace. Good job! Your exercise plan is working.

I'M TOO TIRED NOW, I'LL EXERCISE LATER. Be very wary of this one. It's highly effective because it spares you the guilt that comes with not exercising now but promising to do so later. The problem is that you can fall into a vicious cycle of delays and unfulfilled promises. I know you're tired, but you'll feel better after you exercise. Trust me.

Remember, exercise killers are powerful, and there are many more out there than the ones listed here. Recognize the excuse, and delay it long enough to get your shoes tied. That's half the battle.

Exercise Killers Worksheet

1. I'm too tired to go to the gym today after work. I didn't sleep well last night, and I have to get to bed early tonight.

Counterargument: I'm tired most days, which is why I need to exercise. Plus, I may sleep better tonight after a little exercise.

Evidence supporting your counterargument: The times I force myself to go to the gym when I'm tired, I almost always feel full of energy after I'm done. Also, I slept like a rock 2 nights ago after going to the gym.

How will I overcome this exercise killer? I will remind myself of how I feel after I exercise and how well I sleep after I'm done. I will stop *thinking* about going to the gym and just go.

2. _____

Counterargument: _____

Evidence supporting your counterargument: _____
_____

How will I overcome this exercise killer? _____
_____

List your most common reasons for not exercising, on the Exercise Killers Worksheet, and make an argument for why the excuse is flawed or how you can overcome it. See the example provided; an additional worksheet can be found at http://pubs.apa.org/books/supp/moore.

SUMMARY

Exercise, whether it's walking the dog or running before work, is a great way to prevent and relieve anxiety. Exercise also releases feel-good chemicals in your body, increases self-esteem, and improves physical health. The key is to avoid common exercise excuses, tie your shoes, and take that first step. Here are a few points to take away from this chapter.

- Even a moderate amount of exercise is effective for reducing anxiety.
- Set realistic and specific exercise goals.
- It's easy to talk yourself out of exercising. Pay attention to the excuses you use to avoid exercising.
- Exercise does not have to be boring. The more activities you have in your arsenal, the greater chance of sticking to your routine.
- Starting an exercise routine does not have to be expensive. Avoid the trap of buying needlessly pricey shoes or signing a multiyear contract with a fitness center.

CHAPTER 6

I DON'T HAVE TIME TO RELAX!

The time to relax is when you don't have time for it.
—Sydney J. Harris, American journalist

If you find yourself saying "easier said than done" at some point while reading this book, it will probably be during this chapter. If relaxing were so easy, you wouldn't need to turn to a self-help book, right? The truth is that many of the techniques in this book take work. Some require more time and higher commitment than others. In my opinion, this chapter is one of the easier ones to master. It doesn't take a lot of time. It isn't complicated. And you probably already unknowingly incorporate relaxation into your daily routines. If you walk out to your car after a stressful meeting, take a 15-minute nap during lunch, or have a glass of wine after a hard day at work, then you're using some basic relaxation techniques you've already developed. For some, all it takes is a simple technique during a natural break in the day; for others, relaxing requires a more deliberate and focused effort using newly learned skills. This chapter should help if you fall into the latter group.

Being successful at relaxation requires only two things. First, you must be willing to block out 30 to 45 minutes of your schedule each day. If you can dedicate more time, that's even better. But, drop below 30 minutes, and you likely won't experience any noticeable benefit. Second, and related to the first requirement, you must consistently practice the new techniques. Like most things in life, learning follows repetition. Keep in mind that some of the relaxation techniques may seem awkward in the beginning. You won't find them difficult, but you may feel a bit anxious, especially if you're trying to fit the exercises into an already busy day. You may even feel a bit silly or embarrassed as you learn the new techniques (talk of relaxation exercises often conjures up impressions of mystical forces and new age healers). In my experience with teaching relaxation techniques to patients, the most common obstacle to using the techniques consistently is time. Just as with exercise, watch out for excuses—"I'm too busy," "I forgot," "I've been working more." Such excuses are as common as the winter cold. Don't fall into that trap. If you are serious about getting better at controlling your anxiety, it's important to find a way to ensure your success.

BREATHING

Chances are, you've already got this breathing stuff down pat. How else would you be conscious and able to read this book, right? Breathing is a natural and automatic process. It's something every living being does in some form or fashion. In any given day, the average person takes around 20,000 breaths—that's over 600 million breaths in a lifetime. However, unless it is brought to your attention, breathing usually resides a few steps below your conscious awareness. You barely give this critical, life-sustaining activity the time of day. It's time for that to change. Gaining awareness of your breathing is the first step to using it as an ally against your anxiety. Because you are now aware of your breathing, let's take a closer look at how you breathe.

Chest Versus Diaphragm

Most people are chest breathers. When people inhale, the force of the breath is concentrated in the chest cavity. Chest breathing is a very inefficient method. The lungs are not fully utilized, because of a lack of expansion, which results in less oxygen and nutrients delivered to the blood, brain, and body. This shallow breathing also leads

> Chest breathing is a very inefficient method of breathing.

to an imbalance in oxygen and carbon dioxide levels, which can lead to or worsen anxiety. Common symptoms of prolonged inefficient breathing include dizziness, chest discomfort, and increased heart rate. *Diaphragmatic breathing*, or belly breathing, is a much more efficient way to transfer oxygen and nutrients to the system.

In diaphragmatic breathing, the diaphragm (see illustration), a muscle tightly nestled between the chest and stomach, contracts, forcing your stomach to expand. The force caused by this expansion fills the lungs, leading to maximal oxygen flow to the body. Unlike chest breathing, diaphragmatic breathing promotes a balance of oxygen and carbon dioxide in the body. It also stimulates the parasympathetic nervous system, which is the part of the fight-or-flight system responsible for restoring our body to a normal resting state after a real or perceived threat. Specifically, the parasympathetic system slows down the breathing and heart rate. This balance and restoration are what maintain a relaxed and anxiety-free state. You will learn more about the fight-or-flight system in Chapter 8, on fear. But for now, it's important to remember that it's very difficult for your body to be in an anxious state when you engage in continuous slow and deep breathing.

Learning to Breathe Differently

Becoming a diaphragmatic breather is easy. It involves a few simple steps and requires only minor changes to your daily schedule. The key is to practice the breathing exercise at least two or three times

125

The Diaphragm

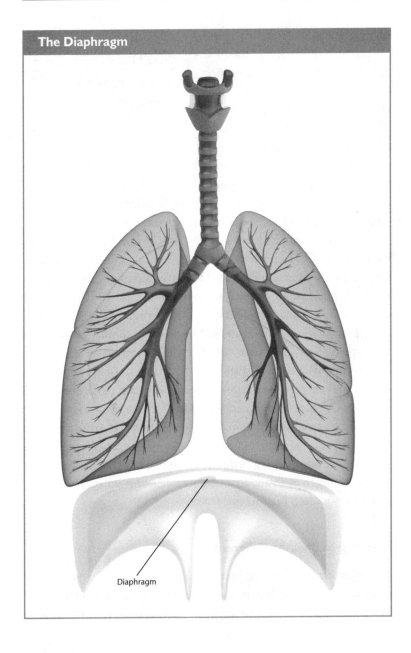

Diaphragm

a day for 15 minutes each time. If you follow this routine, within a couple of weeks you will have trained your body to breathe at a higher level without even knowing it. Here are several variations on the same exercise to get you started.

Diaphragmatic Breathing Exercise—Version 1 (Lying Down)

1. Find a quiet and comfortable place where you can lie down and are guaranteed not to be disturbed for at least 15 minutes. This can be in your bedroom, on the couch in your living room, or in your car with the seat reclined all the way back.

2. With your knees slightly bent and head comfortably supported, place your left hand on your upper chest and your right hand on your stomach. This will help you figure out if you are a chest or diaphragm breather. If you are primarily a chest breather, with each breath the hand on your chest will move while the hand on our stomach remains relatively still. The opposite is true if you are a diaphragm breather. The hand on your stomach will rise while the hand on your chest doesn't. If you are a diaphragm breather, Congratulations! You can move on to the next section. If not, keep reading.

3. Slowly inhale through your nose while consciously making your stomach expand. You should feel the hand on your stomach rise, while the hand on your chest remains still. If you notice that the hand on your chest still moves, continue to focus on making your stomach rise with each inhalation. It may help to picture a deflated balloon as the lining of your relaxed stomach. With each breath you take, visualize the balloon filling with air and your stomach expanding slowly.

4. Slowly exhale through your mouth while tightening your stomach muscles as your stomach slowly returns to its normal

resting place. You should feel the hand on your stomach fall and the hand on your chest should continue to remain still.

5. Repeat this process for 15 minutes at the rate of approximately six full cycles (one cycle per 10 seconds) each minute. Be careful not to rush yourself during the exercise. Your inhalations and exhalations should be slow and smooth.

Diaphragmatic Breathing Exercise—Version 2 (Sitting Up)

1. Find a quiet and comfortable place where you can sit and are guaranteed not to be disturbed for 15 minutes. This can be in a chair or on a couch at home, in your office, or in your car.

2. Sitting comfortably with your legs, shoulders, neck, and head relaxed, place your left hand on your upper chest and your right hand on your stomach. It's important that your body be relaxed and free from muscle tension. The more rigid your body is, the more difficult it is for your diaphragm to expand.

3. Slowly inhale through your nose while consciously making your stomach expand. You should feel the hand on your stomach rise while the hand on your chest remains still. If you notice that the hand on your chest still moves, continue to focus on making your stomach rise with each inhalation. It may help to picture a deflated balloon as the lining of your relaxed stomach. With each breath you take, visualize the balloon filling with air and pushing your stomach outward.

4. Slowly exhale through your mouth while tightening your stomach muscles as your stomach returns to its normal resting place. You should feel the hand on your stomach fall, and the hand on your chest should remain still.

5. Repeat this process for 15 minutes at the rate of approximately five to six full cycles each minute.

Diaphragmatic Breathing Exercise—Version 3[1]

Start by getting comfortable either sitting or lying down. Take a deep breath in through your nose—nice and slow—allowing the air to travel down to your lower abdomen near your belly button. Let your lower abdomen expand as it fills with air. Now gently release your breath, slowly letting the air out of your mouth. Again, slowly breathe in through your nose, and out through your mouth. Many people let some of the air get stuck in their upper chest, but the goal is for the breath to ease down into the lower stomach, without causing the upper chest to rise at all. If this is a challenge for you, try lying down on the floor with a book or a large bag of rice on your upper chest. Practice the calm breathing and try to keep the book still or the bag of rice from rising. That's diaphragmatic breathing in a nutshell. It may sound simplistic, but it's a very effective way of preventing and reducing anxiety. It is also a great way to get through a panic attack or ease nervousness before giving a presentation or getting on a plane. And remember, if you practice diaphragmatic breathing regularly, within a matter of weeks you will retrain your body to breathe this way on its own.

MUSCLE RELAXATION

Whether you know it or not, you're probably walking around with a lot of muscle tension throughout your entire body. For some reason, instead of letting our stress and anxiety go, we store it in our muscles like we store fat in our bellies after bingeing on cookies and ice cream. Intentionally and systematically relaxing

---

[1]From *Relaxation and Wellness Techniques: Mastering the Mind–Body Connection* [CD], by M. Karapetian Alvord, B. Zucker, and B. Alvord. Copyright 2013 by Research Press. Adapted with permission.

your muscles is an excellent way to return your stress and anxiety back to the invisible realm from which it originates. The two best methods for doing this are progressive muscle relaxation and sensation-focused relaxation. Similar to diaphragmatic breathing, both are meant to be practiced at least three times per day for 15 minutes each.

> Stress and anxiety: We store it in our muscles.

Progressive Muscle Relaxation

Developed in the 1930s by Dr. Edmund Jacobson,[2] *progressive muscle relaxation*, or PMR, is a two-step process in which the muscles of the body are intentionally tensed and relaxed. PMR follows a systematic pattern in which you begin with tensing and relaxing the feet and end with the head. The stark contrast between how the muscle feels during contraction and after release is the most important part of the exercise. The main benefits of PMR are that it allows you to experience the positive effects of a relaxed muscle and helps create awareness of what a relaxed muscle typically feels like. The latter allows you to monitor your tension and stress level throughout the day. In essence, worry, fear, stress, and the like have a difficult time winning against a relaxed body. To assist with this exercise, you can download a smartphone app like *Deep Calm—Ambient Sounds to Help You Relax*[3] or *Deep Relax—*

---

[2]Jacobson, E. (1938). *Progressive relaxation*. Chicago, IL: University of Chicago Press.

[3]Imagination Unlimited. (2013). Deep Calm—Ambient Sounds to Help You Relax (Version 1.0.52) [Mobile application software]. Retrieved from https://itunes.apple.com/bz/app/deep-calm-ambient-sounds-to/id700689999?mt=8

Your Best Companion for Stress Relief.[4] Both include a variety of soothing sounds to help you relax.

Progressive Muscle Relaxation Exercise[5]

1. Find a quiet place where you can sit or lie down comfortably and are guaranteed not to be disturbed for 15 minutes.
2. Close your eyes, take a slow deep breath, count to 5, and slowly exhale. Do this five times. (This is a great opportunity to incorporate diaphragmatic breathing into the exercise.)
3. With your feet flat against the ground, shift awareness to either your left or your right foot. Notice the tension in your toes, ankle, sides, bottom, and top of your foot. If your mind wanders and fills with random thoughts, acknowledge them and then gently push them out of your consciousness. It may help to imagine your random thoughts as chalk on a chalkboard, being effortlessly wiped away with an eraser. Continue to breathe.
4. Curl your toes downward and tense your foot as tightly as you can and hold for 5 seconds. Focus only on the tension in your toes and foot. Pay close attention to how it feels.
5. Slowly relax your toes and foot. Notice the relief that results from letting go of the tension. Feel the warm blood rushing back to your toes, foot, and ankle.

---

[4]App Camelot. (2013). Deep Relax—Your Best Companion for Stress Relief (Version 1.4) [Mobile application software]. Retrieved from http://appcamelot.com/app/deep-relax

[5]From *Stress Prevention Activities for Road Transport Drivers and SME: Physical and Physiological Exercises e-learning Module*, by the SPA ROAD project. Copyright 2010 by the Federation of Transport, Communications and Sea workers' General Union of Castile-Leon. Adapted with permission.

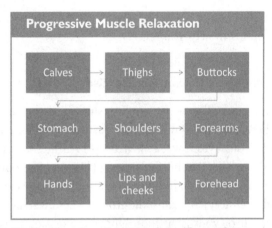

Note. From *Stress Prevention Activities for Road Transport Drivers and SME: Physical and Physiological Exercises e-learning Module*, by the SPA ROAD project. Copyright 2010 by the Federation of Transport, Communications and Sea workers' General Union of Castile-Leon. Adapted with permission.

6. Repeat Steps 3 through 5 two more times while continuing to breathe.
7. Repeat Steps 3 through 6 for the remaining areas of the body as shown in the Progressive Muscle Relaxation diagram.

Sensation-Focused Relaxation

Similar to PMR, sensation-focused relaxation focuses on the various muscles of the body from head to toe (or toe to head). However, instead of tensing and relaxing the muscles, the sensation method focuses on the sensations within the muscles and imagining the tension being washed away. This method combines deep breathing, body awareness, and imagery. Sensation-focused relaxation is no better or worse than PMR—it's just a different approach for reaching the shared goal of relaxation. To assist with this exercise, you can download a smartphone app like *Ocean Wave Sounds for Sleep and Relaxation*[6] or *Sleep Waves*.[7]

Sensation-Focused Relaxation Exercise

1. Find a quiet place where you can sit or lie down comfortably and are guaranteed not to be disturbed for 15 minutes.
2. Close your eyes; take a slow, deep breath; count to 5; and slowly exhale. Do this five times. (Again, this is another great opportunity to incorporate diaphragmatic breathing into a different relaxation strategy.)
3. Shift awareness to either your left or your right foot. Notice the sensations in your toes, ankle, bottom, sides, and top of your foot. If your mind wanders and fills with random thoughts, acknowledge them and then gently push them out of your consciousness. It may help to imagine your random thoughts as clouds breaking apart in the sky and disappearing from sight. Continue to breathe.
4. Imagine warm, soothing, healing water washing over your foot. Feel the water as it envelopes your toes, ankle, top, and sole of your foot. Notice the relief that results from the warm water. Stay focused on this sensation for 2 minutes.
5. Repeat Steps 3 and 4 for the remaining areas of the body as shown in the Progressive Muscle Relaxation diagram while you continue to breathe.

---

[6]Boynes, S. (2013) Ocean Wave Sounds for Sleep and Relaxation (Version 1.3.1) [Mobile application software]. Retrieved from https://itunes.apple.com/us/app/ocean-wave-sounds-for-sleep/id590198818?mt=8
[7]MobileAnarchy. (2012). Sleep Waves (Version 1.0) [Mobile application software]. Retrieved from https://play.google.com/store/apps/details?id=com.mobileanarchy.com.whitenoiseblacknightfree

6. Once you have covered every major muscle group, imagine yourself fully immersed in this water except for your mouth and nose. Focus on how the warmth and weightlessness from floating relaxes your body. Stay with the feeling for as long as you can.

IMAGERY

Guided imagery is a simple, yet effective, way to manage anxiety through directing your imagination. It's used by professional athletes, elite soldiers, cancer patients, and those looking to reduce anxiety and stress. (It is commonly used by children, although it is usually referred to as "daydreaming.") Guided imagery is considered by some as a form of hypnosis. In the traditional sense, a guide (usually a therapist or coach) helps the person access his or her imagery system and suggests visual paths and outcomes related to the reason for employing the imagery. For example, before a big tournament, a professional golfer imagines himself making the perfect swing off the tee, visualizes the ball slicing through the air toward the pin, and watches the ball roll into the hole. He will play this perfect shot over and over again while paying attention to the intricate details of his swing and how his hands feel when the ball meets the sweet spot of his club. He can also visualize and prepare for potential obstacles to making that perfect shot, such as an unexpected gust of wind or a sand trap.

One of the advantages of guided imagery is that you can create a scenario or script to fit your current situation. For example, if you are anxious about an upcoming presentation, you can visualize yourself delivering an award winning talk. If you are afraid of having a panic attack on your next trip to the mall, you can conjure up potential panic triggers (e.g., a large crowd at the food court) and guide yourself to success through playing out different scenarios related to managing your anxiety. Or you can draw upon a favorite memory that makes you feel happy, safe, and relaxed. The great thing about reliving memories is that your mind and body can't discriminate between fantasy and reality. You can recreate those positive feelings purely through imagination. The possibilities are unlimited.

Three different examples of using guided imagery follow. The first is an example of a mother who experiences panic attacks and is anxious about attending her daughter's game. The second deals with a working mom who is under tremendous stress at work and home and needs help relaxing before she even attempts to solve her problems. The third is a general imagery exercise with no particular theme. But before you get started, as with the other relaxation exercises, find a quiet place where you won't be disturbed, close your eyes, and breathe deeply for several minutes.

> You can create a scenario to fit your current situation.

Guided Imagery Example 1: The Big Game

Gracie's daughter is playing in the volleyball state championship game next week. She is excited for her and wants to attend. However, the thought of being around that many cheering and screaming people makes her extremely nervous. She even worries that she will have a panic attack and won't be able to make it out of the gymnasium if one occurs. Gracie's therapist helps her develop the following script:

> Before leaving the house, picture yourself sitting in your car in the parking lot outside of the gymnasium. You are nervous about going inside. Your heart is beating fast, your hands are clammy, and your stomach is in knots. You say to yourself, "I'm going to freak out if I go inside" and "I can't do this."

Now picture yourself using diaphragmatic breathing. Feel your heart rate slowly drop and the discomfort in your abdomen subside. From the car, watch how effortlessly others enter the gymnasium. Remind yourself that you have been to this gymnasium numerous times before and nothing bad ever happened. Picture where you will sit when you enter. Maybe it will be at the end of the bench near the door. Or, maybe you will stand near the concessions counter, which is close to the exit. Remind yourself again that you have done this many times before and you always made it through just fine. Now imagine you are seated and your heart starts to race and you feel the urge to run out the door. You start to question yourself again about whether or not you will be able to handle this sensation. Continue to breathe deeply, and replace the unhelpful thoughts with helpful ones. For example, focus on your daughter and how proud you are of her. Remind yourself that there are exits on both sides of the bleachers in case you will need to leave. Tell yourself you have done this before, and refocus back on your daughter. The anxiety grows, and you are starting to feel overwhelmed. Step outside for a few minutes, but don't go to the car. Breathe, relax, and force out any unhelpful thoughts by telling them to stop. Return to your seat, continue to breathe, and focus on your daughter.

Guided Imagery Example 2: Childhood Memory

Over the past few weeks, life has been hard for Alison. Several work deadlines hit her all at once, her oldest child is in trouble at school, and things haven't been going well between her and her husband. She desperately needs to reduce her emotional and physical stress. Alison's therapist helps her develop the following script:

> Think about Christmas Eve at your grandmother's house when you were 7 years old. Picture yourself standing beside her, helping her peel the apples for the pies she's baking. Notice your grandfather in the background reading a story to your little

brother. Feel the cool, crisp air coming from under the front door and visualize the bright colors of the leaves covering the brown grass outside. Focus on the smell of the turkey as it bastes in the old black iron oven in the corner. Experience each pleasurable thought, feeling, smell, touch, sound, taste, and vision you can conjure up from that day. Remember the joy you felt just being there, wishing that the day would never end. Feel the calmness and contentment that occupied your entire being, and push away any stray thoughts that pop into your head. Try not to think at all. Just imagine yourself being 7 years old again.

General Imagery Exercise[8]

Close your eyes if that helps you to concentrate, or keep them open if you prefer. Get into a comfortable position. You can sit up or lie down. Once you are comfortable, picture a place that you would feel safe and relaxed, and that is free of tension. This can be a real place that you have been to, a place you would like to visit, or a made-up place. It can be indoors, outdoors, or a combination. The power of this exercise is that you decide where you want to go and what it will be like once you are there.

Next, decide what the objects and scenery around you look like. You might be in the woods or mountains or at a beach. You might be aware of a sunrise, sunset, or starry sky. Or you might be inside with furniture that is comfortable and perhaps a fire in the fireplace. Perhaps you are surrounded by books, beautiful art, or painted walls.

Imagine the colors that you associate with tranquility. Many choose blues, greens, and whites, but it can be any color of your choice, or a rainbow of colors. Let those colors surround you.

---

[8]General Imagery Exercise by Mary Karapetian Alvord, PhD, and Kelly A. O'Brien, PhD. Printed with permission.

The temperature is exactly as you like it. There might be a soft or cool breeze, or sun warming your body. Imagine what the air feels like on your skin. Take a deep breath in through your nose so that your abdomen expands; hold it; and slowly, very slowly, breathe out of your mouth. Slowly let your muscles loosen as the tension flows out. Take another deep breath in through your abdomen, hold it, and slowly breathe out of your mouth. With each breath, you release more tension. For some, their body feels heavy as they relax; others feel light. Some sense their muscles warming and others feel cooling or tingling sensations. Become aware of how your body feels as you release the stress and let the tension flow out. Now decide what sounds you would like to hear. You might be aware of a trickle of a stream or ocean waves as they gently break in the sand. Or perhaps you hear birds chirping, wind chimes, or sounds of people in the background, or music. Or, you might prefer silence. Now, imagine the smells that surround you. It might be the smell of something baking in the oven; of scented flowers, such as roses, lilacs, or lavender; the fresh smell of grapefruit or newly cut grass; the familiar smell of a favorite place; a cologne or perfume; or any scent you like. Determine the tastes and textures that you find pleasant: Maybe something crunchy, or something smooth or creamy; something hard or something soft; perhaps salty air, warm or iced flavored tea, the first bite of chocolate chip cookies, or your favorite food. Your mind is free of tension and worry.

Take a deep breath in through your abdomen, hold it, and slowly, very slowly, breathe out any tension left in your body. Simply relax and feel the peace within you and that surrounds you. You may choose to stretch out your fingers and slowly open your eyes or ease into sleep.

One last note. Many people find it useful to record the script on an audio recorder and play it while they relax. Unless you have the script memorized, it can be counterproductive to open your eyes every few seconds to read what comes next. You can download one of several free audio recorders on your smartphone. With that being said, it's also important to be flexible and go with the flow. Your script is your script. You can alter it any way you wish while you are imagining it. Allow the creative parts of your mind to take over.

Summary

Being told to relax is one thing; doing it is something else. Whether you use deep breathing, muscle relaxation, or visualization, these techniques are formidable opponents of anxiety. The key is to practice regularly. Here are a few points to take away from this chapter.

- Slow and focused breathing is a great way to prevent and alleviate anxiety.
- Tensing and relaxing muscles promotes a sense of calmness, relaxation, and contentment.
- Imagery is effective for preventing panic, but it also conjures up positive feelings from past experiences.
- To be effective, relaxation techniques should be used daily for at least 30 to 45 minutes each day.

CHAPTER 7

WHAT DOES IT MEAN TO MANAGE MY ENVIRONMENT?

The secret of all victory lies in the organization of the nonobvious.

—Marcus Aurelius

The idea of "being in control" is often viewed negatively, perhaps because some associate it with "being controlling." When spoken, the phrase "being in control" may bring up thoughts of people who are overbearing, demanding, uncaring, and dismissive. These adjectives may be true for some, particularly those who associate control with getting their way at all costs.

But the truth is that control is a good thing. Control allows you to manage the varying degrees and types of chaos that circle you daily. This is important because chaos is the best friend of anxiety. And feeling out of control is one of the most common complaints from people who suffer from anxiety.

> Chaos is the best friend of anxiety.

As I've mentioned before, life is hectic, and fast paced, and not concerned with how stressed or anxious you are. It doesn't slow down or adjust to make life easier for you. It doesn't appreciate the fact that you have to prepare your presentation tonight while you cook dinner, fold the laundry, empty the dishwasher, and get the kids to bed. It's unaware that you are now having to take care of your sick mother or dealing with the separation from your husband, who is deployed to a combat zone 12,000 miles away. That's why it's important to learn how to control or manage as many things around you as you can. If you don't, your stress and anxiety will grow. The good news is that controlling your environment is not as impossible as it may sound. It's actually quite simple. But it takes effort, some planning, and a bit of patience.

ORGANIZE YOUR SPACE

I used to dread going into work on Mondays. It's not because I didn't like my job or that Monday was any tougher than Tuesday through Friday. It was because my desk was a complete and utter mess. Just as your car gets cluttered on long road trips, my desk suffered the consequences of a week's worth of pulling folders and not putting them back, stacking draft documents in the corner instead of shredding them, and posting sticky notes up and down my office walls. Just looking at the chaos conjured up thoughts such as "I'm never going to get anything done today" and "I just know I'm going to miss a deadline this week." In essence, I started off my week worried and stressed. Fortunately, with the help of a caring and well-organized assistant, this all changed. Whether you work at home or in an office, regardless of whether you're negotiating multimillion dollar contracts or clipping coupons, the following tips that helped me can help you eliminate clutter and reduce stress and anxiety.

MAKE A CLEAN SWEEP. Sometimes you just have to start over. Find a large box, bin, or trashcan and sweep everything off your desk into it. I'm not asking you to throw anything away—yet. Just turn your desk into a blank slate. Once your desk is clean, take a step back and visualize how you'd like it to be. What areas do you want free of clutter? What part of your work area do you tend to use the most? Once you've got a plan in mind, take one thing out of your chosen receptacle and strategically place it back on your desk one piece at a time. As you pull out each object, whether it's a stack of papers, a stapler, or an exceptionally large basket, picture, or radio, ask yourself, "Does this need to be on my desk?" If the answer is no, find a new place for it or do the next step.

Toss, Shred, Recycle, or Store. It's safe to assume that a sizeable portion of the papers, notes, and receipts on your desk serve no real purpose other than to make your desk seem cluttered. Decide what you can toss, shred, or recycle. But don't just stick a to-be-shredded-or-recycled box under your desk—do it immediately. If not, you've done nothing more than move the mess from one spot to another. And for those things that can't be tossed, shredded, or recycled, find a place to store them. Does the cup with a thousand pens really need to be there? Do you need six different pictures of the same person, place, or thing? Can the printer find a home under the desk or on an adjoining table? Find these things new homes.

Develop a Filing System. Sorry, but just putting stuff in a drawer is not filing. You need to develop a sensible system. Create folders and label them clearly. Sort projects and documents by due date, completion status, or importance. Store receipts by year (or month if the Internal Revenue Service makes you nervous). Use bins to store documents related to current and future projects (be careful not to end up with too many bins on your work area). Arrange bills by due dates and coupons by expiration dates. And about those drawers, keep only essential items in them. Plastic spoons, broken paper clips, sugar packets, and discarded pennies have other places they can hang out. During this process, you may realize that you need to invest in a new filing cabinet or bin to house all your stuff. If money is an issue, you can find filing bins starting at around $10 at http://www.amazon.com.

MOVE INTO THE DIGITAL AGE. Now that you have everything in bins, files, and drawers, decide which of these documents can be saved electronically in folders on your computer or other electronic device. One possibility is investing in a digital document scanner. This will allow you to keep all of your important papers and receipts in one place while freeing up space on your desk and in your drawers and cabinets. Document scanners can cost anywhere from $50 to $350.

TIDY UP AT THE END OF EACH DAY. When it's all said and done, if you don't spend a few minutes tidying up at the end of day, you are likely to end up right back where you started. Put things away before you leave the office or when you're done with your work at home. If this is not practical, spend some time at the end of the week organizing your space. You will thank yourself on Monday.

PRIORITIZE AND ACT

You are constantly bombarded with daily tasks that range from minuscule to epic. On any given day, you mentally juggle family, work, and social activities. Responding to these activities haphazardly is a surefire way to get your anxiety and stress level up. Having a systematic plan for how you'll approach your day prevents worrying about whether you're getting everything done that you need to. It also protects you against the fear and panic associated with feeling unprepared. Try the following techniques.

DEVELOP LISTS. In their very practical and useful book, *Attack Your Day! Before It Attacks You*,[1] time management experts Mark

---

[1]Woods, M., & Woods, T. (2012). *Attack your day! Before it attacks you.* Upper Saddle River, NJ: FT Press.

and Trapper Woods recommend the simple act of keeping lists as a way to stay organized. Instead of trying to remember everything in your head, to-do lists help you keep your day, week, and month on track. They allow you to stay organized and reduce the chances that you'll forget something. According to Mark and Trapper, three types of lists are most useful for getting organized.

- First, there's the *daily* list. The daily list helps you keep track of—you guessed it—what you need to do today. It's nothing more than a list of tasks you brainstorm at the beginning of the day or the day before. As you complete a task, you simply cross it off your list. Examples of a task on your daily list may include picking up your child after soccer practice or picking up the dry cleaning.
- The second type of list is the *weekly* list. This list allows you to keep the important deadlines of the week front and center on your dashboard. Throughout the week you can monitor the progress you've made on each task. The weekly tasks are usually more general in nature than the daily ones. Examples of a task on your weekly list may include scheduling a time to talk with your boss or calling the plumber to come out and fix a leaky faucet.
- The third type of list is your *monthly* list. In essence, this is your monthly planner that helps you forecast important meetings, activities, and deadlines for the near future. Examples include changing the oil in your car or cleaning the rain gutters on your house.

There's no need to get fancy with these to-do lists. A standard legal pad will suffice. Or, if you are more technologically inclined, you can use the calendar on your computer or smartphone. You may find the smartphone apps Errands To-Do List,[2] Week Planner—Fast and Simple,[3] and Everyday Notes Monthly[4] helpful.

BRING SOME COLOR INTO YOUR LIFE. Another useful and very simple activity recommended by Mark and Trapper is the practice of color coding your time. Color coding your schedule is a great way to keep the most important items of your day and week in plain sight. Although you can choose any colors you like, they recommend red, green, yellow, and gray. You guessed it: Red means *Stop! Do now*. These are the things that can't wait, such as picking up the kids from school, attending an urgent meeting, or calling the credit card company to find out why your card was declined at the grocery store. Green stands for *Go*. Green tasks are the bread and butter of your day: balancing the budget, preparing for a presentation later in the week, and setting up a business meeting. The goal is to get as many green tasks done during the day as you can. The world won't stop if you don't get to them all, but greens can easily turn to reds. So be careful. Yellow activities are those of low importance but that eventually have to get done: cleaning out your closet, pulling weeds from the flower bed, and making lunch plans with a friend. And then there are the grays. Gray activities are wastes of time and should be avoided unless you are completely caught up with everything else. Examples include watching television and surfing the Internet.

DON'T PROCRASTINATE. American writer Mason Cooley once said, "Procrastination makes easy things hard, hard things harder." Pro-

---

[2]Yoctoville. (2013) Errands To-Do List (Version 4.0.2) [Mobile application software]. Retrieved from http://yoctoville.com

[3]Easun. (2011). Week Planner—Fast and Simple (Version 1.1) [Mobile application software]. Retrieved from http://blog.naver.com/belly3k

[4]Adylitica. (2013). Everyday Notes Monthly (Version 2.0.7) [Mobile application software]. Retrieved from http://tomorrow.do/

crastination is a fierce enemy of productivity. If you want to conquer this foe, you must follow three simple steps. First, don't think, just do. Just like with exercise, once you start telling yourself how difficult or unpleasant it will be, you are less likely to do it. Second, the more unpleasant a task is, the earlier you should do it. Difficult and tedious tasks are easier to do when your brain and body are rested. Put them off until the end of the day and, well, good luck. Chances are you will talk yourself into doing them tomorrow. Third, reward yourself after a victory, no matter how small. Take a 5-minute break. Chat with a friend or colleague. Reinforce your perseverance and sacrifice by taking yourself out to lunch or for a cup of coffee.

LEARN TO DELEGATE

Delegating tasks to others is a great way to reduce your anxiety. Granted, although you may worry about whether the person you've delegated will actually complete the task, the pressure for you to juggle countless responsibilities throughout the day is reduced. In turn, you're more efficient, feel less stressed, and avoid the unwelcome anxiety associated with the constant thought of "how am I going to get everything done?" Here are a few delegation tips to get you going.

LEARN TO LET GO. You first need to let go of the notion that you and only you can correctly do what needs to be done. This world is filled with lots of competent people. Trust that those around you, whether it's your spouse, child, parent, or coworker, are able to ease your burden. (Of course, whether they're willing to is a different story!) Just let go of your need to control the small things in life.

CHOOSE THE RIGHT PERSON. Before you start dishing out responsibilities, figure out what you think you need to do versus what others can do. For example, if asking your husband to pick up the kids after school will cause you to worry all day, then you may want to hang on to this task. Asking him to pick up the dry cleaning may be a better option. The goal is to let go of time-intensive tasks that will have minimal consequences if they're not done while maintaining control of those responsibilities deemed to be highest priority.

BE SPECIFIC. People do better when they know exactly what's expected. When you delegate something to someone else, make sure to spell out exactly what it is you need help with. For example, instead of saying, "Can you take care of the kitchen tonight?" say, "Can you unload the dishwasher, wipe down the cabinets, and take out the trash?" Instead of saying, "Can you help with the kids?" say, "Can you give them their baths tonight?" Just be clear, direct, and specific. One other thing: Don't forget to thank the people who have helped you when they're done. This is a great way to make sure they help out again in the future.

FOLLOW-UP. If you want to make sure something doesn't get done, assign a task and forget about it. An important part of delegating responsibility is to follow up and make sure the task is completed. Remember, you are still in charge of the task and have entrusted someone else to execute it for you. People are more likely to come through when they know someone's going to check on the final product. However, this doesn't mean being a tyrant. A good manager always treats his or her employees with respect, patience, and understanding.

GIVE PRAISE. This is Psychology 101. Praise is highly reinforcing. All it takes is a simple "thank you" or "you're a big help" to keep the pipeline of assistance open. If

Praise is highly reinforcing.

you're harsh or overly critical, it's less likely that the person will help you down the road.

PENCIL IN SOME "ME" TIME

In the movie *The Shining*,[5] Jack Nicholson emblazoned the proverb "All work and no play makes Jack a dull boy" into our collective consciousness. There is quite a bit of truth to this age-old saying. However, a more appropriate version for today's society may be "All work and no play makes Jack or Jane an anxious girlfriend, father, employee, friend" and so on. Working hard is good. It makes you feel worthwhile and instills a sense of pride. But if you are always on your smartphone or spend more time at committee meetings than with your family, your life will quickly become chaotic and seem out of control. A great equalizer to the stress and strain associated with today's fast-paced world is having fun. Sometime between childhood and now, you've forgotten how important playtime is for your emotional health. It's time to get back to your childhood roots.

FIGURE OUT WHAT YOU LIKE TO DO. You'd be surprised, but a sizeable portion of people can't tell you what they like to do for fun. Give it some thought. Do you like to go on hikes, ride bicycles, visit museums or amusement parks, go antiquing, or hit the neighborhood garage sales? Do you like to spend time alone, with family, friends, or perfect strangers? Decide how often you'll do your chosen activity (daily, weekly, monthly, yearly) and choose an activity or activities that you'll actually do. Traveling across Europe or climbing the Himalayas may not be practical. Use the

---

[5]Kubrick, S. (Producer & Director). (1980). *The shining* [Motion picture]. United States: Warner Bros.

Figure out what you like to do.

following chart to help you decide. The first one has been done for you. You can find a blank Recreation Decision Log at http://pubs.apa.org/books/supp/moore.

SCHEDULE FUN TIME. Just like how financial advisors tell you to pay yourself first, you should also schedule your leisure time first. Take a look at your daily, weekly, or monthly schedule. Pencil in your chosen activity before you schedule anything else. Make meetings, errands, and all other responsibilities revolve around your leisure time. Following is a daily planner you can use to pencil in some fun (depending on your activity, a weekly or monthly planner may be more appropriate). You can also find the Recreation Planner at http://pubs.apa.org/books/supp/moore.

MAKE LEISURE A PRIORITY. The hard part is over. You've decided what you want to do and when you want to do it. Now you just have to do it. Unfortunately, this is the step where things tend to go south for a lot of people. You've gone through the trouble of getting this far, so make fun a priority. Don't bump it from your schedule for a meeting or errand that can wait. You have to change how you view leisure time. Fun is not optional—it's a requirement, just like going to work, school, or cooking dinner.

TAKE A VACATION. A vacation is a nice way to enjoy yourself while getting away from the hassles of daily life. Again, you don't have to tromp around Europe for 2 weeks. A vacation can simply be a day at the park with your family or an overnight getaway at a bed-and-breakfast an hour from your home. These are called "staycations," and they allow you to break away from the monotony and grind of everyday life without breaking the bank.

Recreation Decision Log

Activity	Why this activity?	Alone/someone else?	Likelihood of doing it? (1–10).	Barriers? Solution?
Go to estate sales.	I enjoy shopping and it's a great way to get nice items for the house at a good price.	I think my husband would enjoy going with me.	6	Money has been tight lately. I can go and just browse.

Recreation Planner

TIME	Monday	Tuesday	Wednesday	Thursday	Friday	Saturday	Sunday
5:00 a.m.							
5:30							
6:00							
6:30							
7:00							
7:30							
8:00							
8:30							
9:00							
9:30							
10:00							
10:30							
11:00							
11:30							
12:00							
12:30							

1:00								
1:30								
2:00								
2:30								
3:00								
3:30								
4:00								
4:30								
5:00								
5:30								
6:00								
6:30								
7:00								
7:30								
8:00								
8:30								
9:00								
9:30 p.m.								

REDUCE THE NOISE

Anxious people tend to be hypersensitive to noise. This hypersensitivity may be related to noise that triggers an unpleasant memory in someone who experienced a past trauma. Or it may be noise that fuels a sense of being out of control, agitation, or tension in someone who's already anxious. Regardless, there are benefits to reducing the constant buzzing, clattering, and clamoring around you.

TURN OFF THE TELEVISION. Even when you are not watching television, my guess is that you still have it on. Just like traffic, sirens, and barking dogs, television has become an acceptable source of background noise in your life. Simple fix. If you're not watching television, turn it off. Not only will you reduce your electric bill, you'll also reduce your stress and anxiety. If you are someone who finds the background noise of the television comforting, try turning it down.

TURN OFF THE CELL PHONE. I understand that turning your phone off may not be practical. You don't want to miss an important call. But at least turn it off for dinner or during conversations. Or keep the ringer on vibrate. Believe it or not, people used to make it through the day without answering phone calls and texts every 15 minutes.

GET RID OF ALERTS. Do you really need a Tweet, bong, or 3-second clip from a Barry Manilow song going off every time you get a friend update, text message, or e-mail? Alerts signal urgency and are meant for more serious things like fires and tornadoes. Unless you have some reason to suspect your friend will be caught in either, turn them off.

SCHEDULE QUIET TIME. Sometimes you can't stop the noise. You can, however, remove yourself from it. Schedule a time during the day when you can get away and enjoy the natural benefits of silence. If nothing else, wear headphones or earplugs to drown out the auditory chaos around you.

COMMUNICATE MORE EFFECTIVELY

Although it may not seem like it at times, you have quite a bit of control over how conversations with loved ones turn out. When conversations turn out badly, your anxiety will increase. Therefore, managing this important aspect of your life effectively will pay dividends for your emotional health. In his book *Roadmap to Resilience*,[6] Dr. Donald Meichenbaum, prominent psychologist and cofounder of cognitive behavior therapy, provides several tips on how to effectively communicate with your partner.[7]

- Show genuine interest in what the other person is saying. Try to understand your partner's point of view.
- Respond to what your partner says. There is nothing more frustrating than being ignored when you are sharing your feelings and thoughts.
- Accept your partner's perspective. You don't have to agree with it, but show it the respect it deserves.
- At all costs, don't interrupt and don't finish your partner's sentences. Wait until he or she has finished talking.
- Encourage your partner to speak freely and to feel safe expressing his or her feelings and thoughts.

---

[6]Meichenbaum, D. (2012). *Roadmap to resilience: A guide for military, trauma victims, and their families*. Clearwater, FL: Institute Press.

[7]Meichenbaum, D. (2012). *Roadmap to resilience: A guide for military, trauma victims, and their families* (pp. 49–50). Clearwater, FL: Institute Press.

At the risk of being cliché, communication is not a one-way street. It requires cooperation, understanding, and above all, respect for the person you're communicating with. And for most of us, effective communication doesn't come naturally. To become good at it requires deliberate effort and thoughtfulness. But if you master it, you will gain more control over your environment and your anxiety. For more information on effective communication, particularly as it relates to being assertive, see Chapter 9.

SUMMARY

In today's world, staying organized is a challenge. You are forced to juggle countless responsibilities that require constant attention. Learning to work smart as opposed to working hard is key to reducing the chaos that surrounds you. Here are a few points to take away from this chapter.

- Maintaining control can help you stay grounded and productive and reduce your stress.
- Technology can help you organize your life and reduce your anxiety.
- Creating and prioritizing your to-do lists and learning to better manage your time will help you be efficient and effective with your responsibilities, and, in turn, reduce your anxiety.
- People often overlook the importance of having fun. Schedule leisure time into your day, week, and month.
- Excessive background noise and e-mail and phone alerts lead to distraction and stress.

CHAPTER 8

CAN'T I JUST STAY AWAY
FROM THE THINGS I FEAR?

*Most of our obstacles would melt away if, instead of cowering
before them, we should make up our minds to walk boldly
through them.*

—Orison Swett Marden, American author
and founder of *Success* magazine

What does fear have in common with joy, sadness, anger, contempt,
disgust, and surprise? It's one of the basic human emotions. In contrast to learned emotions, such as guilt and shame, fear is with people at birth and possibly even before. Unpleasant as it is, fear serves
a valuable purpose: It keeps you safe. Without it, you might find
yourself wandering into a bear's den, jumping into shark-infested
waters, or rappelling down a 20-story building on nothing more
than a dare and a frayed rope. In fact, fear has played a critical role
in human evolution.

FIGHT OR FLIGHT

The *fight-or-flight response* is the physiological and behavioral consequence of fear. Hardwired into people's genetic makeup and passed
down by ancestors, this innate mechanism prepares people to defend
(fight) or flee (flight) when faced with a threat—a very handy thing
to have when our ancestors came face-to-face with a woolly mam-
moth. Comprising two counterbalanced parts, the sympathetic and
parasympathetic nervous systems, the fight-or-flight response regulates
stress chemicals in the body. These chemicals cause a number of highly

adaptive bodily processes to occur when threatened (see the following Threat System figure). Once the threat is gone, the system returns a person back to his or her original resting state. But like most delicately balanced systems, things can and do go awry, as is the case in certain types of anxiety, such as panic attacks, phobias, and posttraumatic stress. Fear, as well as its physiological and behavioral consequences, becomes associated with nonthreatening situations, events, memories, people, and things. Or in the case of panic disorder, panic attacks come out of the blue. For whatever reason, in panic disorder, people's internal biological wires get crossed, leading to unpredictable bursts of fear. Regardless of whether people see it coming or not, fear causes significant emotional distress for the person experiencing it.

AVOID AVOIDANCE

Ironically, the best way to overcome your fear is to face it head on. Sounds easy enough, right? The problem is that purposefully confronting danger is in direct opposition to what your body and mind want to do. In fact, your body and mind desperately want to avoid the threat at all costs. This makes sense, especially when the threat is real. But in people with chronic anxiety, avoidance of fear is highly reinforcing. For example, if you get anxious going to restaurants, staying home to avoid the anxiety reinforces your behavior of staying home. Consequently, the next time someone asks you to lunch, you are more likely to decline. If you are afraid of passing out from a panic attack while walking through the mall, you will likely avoid the mall (and maybe other places where crowds gather). Although avoidance provides immediate and substantial psychological benefits, the long-term effects can vary from annoying to devastating. Passing on a few lunch dates or skipping a shopping trip or two is generally not a big deal. Never leaving the house because you want to completely avoid being in public is a different matter.

The 'fight or flight' response gets the body ready to fight or run away. Once a threat is detected your body responds automatically. All of the changes happen for good reasons, but may be experienced as uncomfortable when they happen in 'safe' situations.

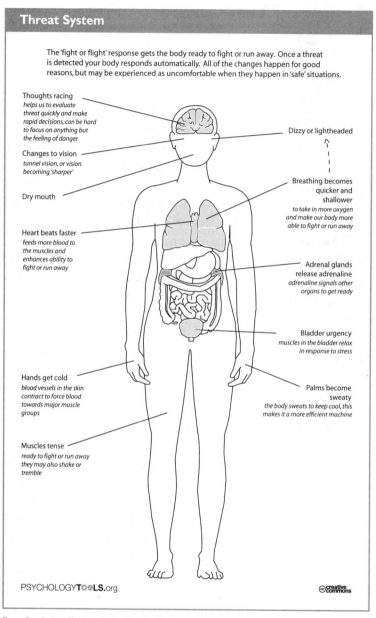

Thoughts racing
helps us to evaluate threat quickly and make rapid decisions, can be hard to focus on anything but the feeling of danger

Changes to vision
tunnel vision, or vision becoming 'sharper'

Dry mouth

Heart beats faster
feeds more blood to the muscles and enhances ability to fight or run away

Hands get cold
blood vessels in the skin contract to force blood towards major muscle groups

Muscles tense
ready to fight or run away they may also shake or tremble

Dizzy or lightheaded

Breathing becomes quicker and shallower
to take in more oxygen and make our body more able to fight or run away

Adrenal glands release adrenaline
adrenaline signals other organs to get ready

Bladder urgency
muscles in the bladder relax in response to stress

Palms become sweaty
the body sweats to keep cool, this makes it a more efficient machine

PSYCHOLOGY**T**●●**LS**.org

creative commons

From PsychologyTools website. Reprinted with permission.

The best way to overcome your fear is to face it head on.

My point is that occasionally avoiding a situation that makes you anxious is fine. It becomes a problem when the avoidance develops into a pattern that has a negative effect on your relationships, work, school, and/or overall satisfaction with life. Often, the latter requires professional help (see Chapter 10 of this book). Although not a substitute for seeking the services of a mental health professional, the tips and techniques below can help.

Awareness is the first step in overcoming life challenges. Therefore, recognizing when you avoid people, places, or things as a way to keep anxiety at arm's length is key. Once you are able to identify your anxiety-avoiding behavior, you can do something about it. The following three tips will help you gain awareness about your avoidance.

BE AWARE OF YOUR FEELINGS. Anxious feelings are generally the first indicator that something is wrong. Maybe you feel a little uneasy or nervous. Or you may have a vague sense that something bad is about to happen. Feelings are a great reminder that you may be avoiding something very soon.

BE AWARE OF YOUR THOUGHTS. Listening to what you say to yourself is a great way to gain awareness that you are about to engage in avoidance as a way to fend off anxiety. Statements such as "I need to get out of here," "Something doesn't feel right," and "I don't need to do this" are common examples. When you have those thoughts, try to figure out what's fueling them. Did someone just say something that was upsetting to you? Did you see something that startled you?

BE AWARE OF YOUR BEHAVIOR. Do you find yourself standing next to the door in social situations? Do you drive only during the very early or late hours of the day? Do you avoid taking new projects at work that require presenting to or speaking in front of a group? Maintaining constant awareness of your behavior allows you to recognize things you do and don't do to keep anxiety at bay.

PHOBIAS

Phobias are a common source of anxiety for many people; estimates are that as many as one in 10 people experience a phobia.[1] In fact, just about everyone experiences some level of discomfort associated with at least one object, place, or situation at some point during his or her life. Aversion to noxious things is adaptive, as is avoidance: It keeps us safe, and it dates back to humans' early ancestors, who were forced to adapt to harsh and inhospitable environments. It was this learned fear of certain reptiles, insects, animals, poisonous plants, and heights by our ancestors that enabled us to exist today.

There are more than 500 documented phobias.[2] The most common ones include fear of animals (e.g., snakes, dogs), insects (mosquitos), blood/injections (seeing blood or getting a shot), heights, flying, public speaking, and death. However, it's important to remember that less than 10% of people actually have a diagnosable phobic disorder. But, as I mentioned above, most people experience some degree of discomfort when confronted with a dangerous or just plain creepy person, place, or thing. The impact on their life is just not as severe as it is with someone who has a disorder.

Phobias develop from learning. At some point, the person who has a phobia has learned to associate anxiety with some object,

---

[1]National Institute of Mental Health. (n.d.) *Specific phobia among adults.* Retrieved from http://www.nimh.nih.gov/statistics/1SPEC_ADULT.shtml

[2]Culbertson, F. (1995). *The phobia list.* Retrieved from www.phobialist.com

person, place, or situation. For example, a child who is bitten by a dog may develop a phobia to dogs later in life. After being a passenger on an unusually bumpy and scary flight, a man may develop a fear of flying. A woman who was assaulted in an underground parking garage may develop a fear of dark and enclosed spaces. And, there is the learning that has been passed down to us by our ancestors through our genes: For example, few people have ever been bitten by a snake, but many fear them. Most of us have never fallen from a tall building, but our knees buckle when we look over the railing at the top of a skyscraper. In essence, an extreme and usually unrealistic fear is associated with something, which causes the person to avoid that something at all costs. The physical and emotional reactions are often extreme. In some cases, the person will have a full-blown panic attack when confronted with the phobic object or situation. This is problematic for the businessman who needs to travel for work, the child who lives in a neighborhood with a lot of dogs, and the woman whose office building has an underground parking garage.

HOW EXPOSURE CAN HELP YOU GET
THE BEST OF FEAR AND PHOBIAS

As common and distressing as phobias are, they respond very well to treatment. Specifically, *exposure therapy* is considered the gold standard by mental health professionals. Popularized in the middle part of the 20th century by psychologist Joseph Wolpe,[3] exposure therapy allows a person to face his or her fears in a controlled and

---

[3]Wolpe, J. (1969). *The practice of behavioral therapy.* New York, NY: Pergamon.

supportive environment. By gradually confronting feared objects, paired with the use of relaxation exercises, the therapist helps the person reduce the fear associated with the object.

Although professional help is often needed, self-help strategies are very useful for phobias as well. One of the more helpful ones is *graded exposure*. Graded exposure involves constructing a hierarchy of feared objects or situations from least to most feared. The individual then confronts the feared objects or situations in a gradual or stepwise progression. As opposed to jumping in all at once and becoming overwhelmed with anxiety, the person is able to gradually reduce the fear by confronting situations in a manner that provokes increasing levels of anxiety. The goal is to experience the anxiety associated with the object or situation long enough for the anxiety to go away or to be significantly reduced. Once that occurs, you move on to the next activity until you reach the top of your hierarchy. Generally, the Fear Hierarchy ranges from 1 to 10, with 1 being the *least feared* and 10 being the *most feared*.

It is important to set yourself up for success. Instead of starting off with an object or situation at the top of your Fear Hierarchy, you should begin with an activity that has a stress level somewhere in the middle. For example, you may want to start off at a Level 5. If you find that this is too difficult, you can drop to a Level 4, 3, and so on. If you find that your Level 5 is too easy, you may want to reconsider and reorganize your hierarchy. It's important to remember that the goal is to experience discomfort long enough for your body and mind to become used to the anxiety associated with the behavior. This can be difficult, but that's the point. If at any time you feel that the activity is too overwhelming, drop down a notch or two on your hierarchy. If you find yourself wanting to stop the exercise, that's okay. People's normal inclination is to stop doing something that causes them distress. But do your best to fight the urge to stop. The only way exposure can work is if you experience the anxiety

Fear Hierarchy for Going out in Public

Identify 10 activities that cause you anxiety related to your fear. Rank the distress level from 10 (*most distress*) to 1 (*least distress*); use 5 as a medium level of distress.

Activity	Level of distress
Eating at the mall food court during the lunch hour	10 (*most*)
Going into the mall and walking to the food court and back	9
Driving to the mall and sitting in your car	8
Going into a local store, making a purchase, and talking with the cashier	7
Going into a local store and walking from one end to the other	6
Driving to a local store but staying in the car	5 (*medium*)
Walking over to a neighbor's house and having a brief conversation	4
Walking to your mailbox and back	3
Imagining yourself going to the food court in the mall	2
Imagining yourself going shopping at a store near your home	1 (*least*)

long enough that it loses its intensity and hold on you. If you need to, pause and use one of the relaxation exercises you learned earlier. Once you've recovered, start the exercise again. Included are two examples. The first is a Fear Hierarchy of someone who has a fear of going out in public. The second deals with someone who has a fear of public speaking. You can find a blank Fear Hierarchy table at http://pubs.apa.org/books/supp/moore.

Fear Hierarchy for Public Speaking

Identify 10 activities that cause you anxiety related to your fear. Rank the distress level from 10 (*most distress*) to 1 (*least distress*); use 5 as a medium level of distress.

Activity	Level of distress
Giving a 15-minute speech to a large audience	10 (*most*)
Giving a 5-minute speech to a small group	9
Introducing someone in front of a large audience	8
Telling a joke or story in a small group of people you don't know	7
Giving a brief, informal presentation at work	6
Volunteering for a brief, informal presentation at work	5 (*medium*)
Giving a 2-minute speech in front of family/friends	4
Reading a newspaper article in front of family/friends	3
Watching someone giving a presentation; imagine yourself doing it	2
Talking to a friend about how you would feel giving a speech	1 (*least*)

A Word of Caution

Graded exposure is a difficult exercise. Instead of using the technique alone, I strongly recommend you find a fear partner to help. For some people, excessive levels of anxiety can cause lightheadedness, dizziness, and fainting. If you are one of those people, using the technique without a support person puts you at risk of injuring yourself from a fall. One option is to make overcoming your fear a family affair: Consider enlisting a family member or friend who can provide you with physical support if needed during the exercise, and emotional support as well. However, it's important to choose someone who will not let you off easy. The natural inclination of our loved ones is to protect us from those things that cause us distress. You want them to support you, not rescue you from your fear.

APPLIED TENSION FOR BLOOD AND NEEDLE PHOBIAS

Many people get queasy at the sight of blood or needles. For some, the reaction is extreme. Upon exposure, those with a blood or needle phobia may experience lightheadedness, dizziness, and even fainting. Passing out at the sight of blood or from an injection is not very common. But when it does happen, it's frightening for the person and those around.

The symptoms associated with a blood or needle phobia are caused by a quick drop in heart rate and blood pressure. This may sound counter to what you've already learned about anxiety, which is that anxiety causes your heart rate and blood pressure to increase. In blood and needle phobias, immediately before the trigger (seeing blood, receiving an injection), heart rate and blood pressure do increase. However, within a matter of seconds, they quickly drop. As a result of decreased heart rate and blood pressure, blood flow to the brain is reduced, leading to lightheadedness, dizziness, nausea, and fainting. Called the *vasovagal response*, this process results from excessive stimulation of the vagus nerve, which is responsible for regulating heart rate among other bodily functions. Rarely are any serious or permanent injuries associated with a vasovagal episode. However, injuries tend to be caused by falling after fainting, which is why it's important to always be seated or lying down if you have a blood or needle phobia and to let your doctor, nurse, or lab technician know that you are prone to vasovagal syncope (fainting).

The most effective treatment for a blood or needle phobia is *applied tension*. Applied tension is an easy way to teach yourself how to intentionally increase your blood pressure immediately preceding or during a triggering event. By increasing your blood pressure, you can prevent fainting or, at a minimum, decrease the time it takes you to recover after fainting. For example, before giving blood or getting a shot, you can purposefully increase your blood pressure before the needle stick. This will help protect you from having your pressure drop too low. Or, if after you've been stuck, you start feeling lightheaded and dizzy, you can increase your blood pressure, which will counter your faint feeling. Follow these instructions for using applied tension.[4]

1. Find a quiet and comfortable place you can sit or lie down. Tense the muscles in your arms, legs, and torso for 15 seconds or until you feel a warm feeling in your face and head. Relax for 20 seconds and repeat the step five more times.
2. Repeat Step 1 at least five times a day, each day for an entire week. If possible, practice the same time every day in the same position (seated or lying). The goal is for the practice to become automatic. You not only want to prevent your vasovagal symptoms from occurring, you want to be able to fight them off when they do occur.
3. Develop a Fear Hierarchy like the one shown previously. Ranging from 1 to 10, construct a stressful blood and/or needle hierarchy of triggering objects, events, or situations. Gradually expose yourself to these objects, events, or situations similar to the following example. Use the applied tension technique to counter the effects of reduced heart rate and blood pressure.

---

[4]Davey, G., Cavanagh, K., Jones, F., Turner, L., & Whittington, A. (2012). *Managing anxiety with CBT for dummies*. West Sussex, England: Wiley.

A Word of Caution

Just like with exposure, instead of using applied tension alone, I strongly recommend you find someone to help you. In fact, I don't recommend you use this technique without someone nearby to catch you if you fall. Fainting is a real possibility, which can lead to injury.

Remember, you want to start off with an activity that is in the medium difficulty range. Engage in the activity until your anxiety disappears or drops to a level you can manage. Then move up the fear ladder until you reach your Level 10.

Fear Hierarchy for a Needle Phobia

Identify 10 activities that cause you anxiety related to your fear. Rank the distress level from 10 (*most distress*) to 1 (*least distress*); use 5 as a medium level of distress.

Activity	Level of distress
Getting an injection or giving blood	10 (*most*)
Pricking your finger with a sterile needle	9
Holding a needle or syringe in your hand	8
Touching a needle or syringe	7
Watching someone getting an injection or giving blood	6
Watching a video of someone getting an injection or giving blood	5 (*medium*)
Looking at a real picture of a needle or syringe	4
Looking at a cartoon picture of a needle or syringe	3
Talking with someone about getting an injection or giving blood	2
Thinking about getting an injection or giving blood	1 (*least*)

SUMMARY

Phobias are a common occurrence. The most common ones include fear of snakes, animals, public speaking, heights, and blood/needles. These constitute only a small fraction, however, of the 500 or so phobias that have been documented. Phobias can be treated effectively; in many cases professional treatment is needed. In some cases, however, simple self-help techniques can be used to manage the fear. Here are a few points to take away from this chapter.

- Fear serves a purpose: It protects people from real threats. Fear becomes a problem when it occurs in the absence of a threat or affects quality of life.
- Avoidance reinforces fear and anxiety.
- The goal of graded exposure is to confront anxiety in a stepwise fashion and experience the anxiety until the severity is reduced to a manageable level.
- You should rely on a support person when attempting exposure techniques outside of the therapist's office.

CHAPTER 9

HOW CAN I TAKE CONTROL OF PANIC BEFORE IT TAKES CONTROL OF ME?

We experience moments absolutely free from worry. These brief respites are called panic.

—Cullen Hightower

Panic attacks are one of the most common anxiety complaints across all cultures. It's estimated that one in three people will experience a panic attack at some point in his or her life. For those who experience them, panic attacks are often considered the most distressing of all the anxiety symptoms. Characterized by periods of intense fear or apprehension, panic attacks appear suddenly, often without any warning. The person experiences a feeling of dread, impending doom, suffocation, and even a sense of dying. Thoughts like "I'm going crazy" or "I'm losing it" are common. There are a number of distressing physical sensations as well. During a panic attack, a person may report a racing heart, sweating, trembling, shortness of breath, dizziness, nausea, and numbness (see Chapter 4 for a more comprehensive list). Reports of chest pain are also common, leading some to believe they are having a heart attack. Ironically, normal and harmless physical sensations often jump-start a panic episode. The person may interpret a slight twinge, ache, or flutter as a sign of an impending attack, which then leads to one. In approximately 3% of people, repeated panic attacks and anticipatory anxiety about having future attacks generally lead to a diagnosis of

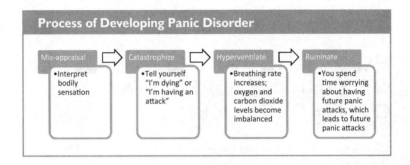

Process of Developing Panic Disorder

Mis-appraisal	Catastrophize	Hyperventilate	Ruminate
•Interpret bodily sensation	•Tell yourself "I'm dying" or "I'm having an attack"	•Breathing rate increases; oxygen and carbon dioxide levels become imbalanced	•You spend time worrying about having future panic attacks, which leads to future panic attacks

panic disorder.[1] Although the process of developing panic disorder is complicated, the Process of Developing Panic Disorder diagram provides a basic explanation. Panic attacks associated with panic disorder are different than those associated with a phobia. There are specific triggers with phobias (e.g., seeing a snake, giving a speech). Outside of benign physical sensations, there is generally no identifiable trigger in panic disorder.

WHAT CAUSES PANIC?

The sympathetic and parasympathetic nervous systems are responsible for panic attacks. As discussed in Chapter 8, these systems oversee numerous functions, which prepare you for action when confronted with a threat and return you to a resting state when the threat is gone. The fight-or-flight response is the main component of these systems. Since the beginning of humankind, this system has served as an internal warning system that keeps humans safe from dangers in the environment. In panic attacks, and in panic disorder

---

[1]National Institute of Mental Health. (n.d.). *The numbers count: Mental disorders in America.* Retrieved from http://www.nimh.nih.gov/health/publications/the-numbers-count-mental-disorders-in-america/index.shtml#Panic

in particular, there is a misfiring in the nervous system, leading to feelings of threat when there is none.

At the onset of fear, several physiological processes occur. First, the hormone epinephrine, also referred to as adrenaline, is dumped into the bloodstream by the adrenal glands. This leads to the symptoms of a racing heart, sweating, and shortness of breath. Second, carbon dioxide levels in the body drop, because of an increased rate of breathing. This leads to feelings of lightheadedness, numbness, twitching, and flushed skin. And last, epinephrine causes the blood vessels in the body to constrict. This leads to chills, dizziness, and fainting.

> An adrenaline surge leads to a racing heart, sweating, and shortness of breath.

TECHNIQUES FOR CONTROLLING PANIC

Panic attacks and panic disorder can be effectively treated with both psychotherapy and medication, with psychotherapy being the most effective.[2] However, a number of self-help techniques can help you reduce, manage, and even eliminate your panic. Following are a few of the most useful ones.

Psychoeducation

When it comes to panic attacks, knowledge is power. Understanding what panic attacks are, why they occur, and how to overcome them can be extremely therapeutic. In addition to what you've

---

[2]Charney, M. E., Kredlow, M. A., Bui, E., & Simon, N. M. (2013). Panic disorder. In S. M. Stahl & B. A. Moore (Eds.), *Anxiety disorders: A guide for integrating psychopharmacology and psychotherapy* (pp. 201–220). New York, NY: Routledge Press.

already learned about the fight-
or-flight response and the causes
and symptoms of panic attacks,

> Panic never killed anyone.

the following information is important for managing your anxiety.

Panic Never Killed Anyone. It may feel like you are going to die, but panic attacks have never sent anyone to an early grave. The chest pain, shortness of breath, and tingling are nothing more than chemicals altering physiological processes in your body. You are not having a heart attack, suffocating, or going to pass out.

Panic Attacks Are Brief. The distress associated with panic attacks generally reaches its peak within 10 minutes. In fact, panic episodes often resolve within a few minutes. That doesn't mean you won't feel the effects long after the attack is over; many people report feeling uneasy or upset 30 to 60 minutes afterward. But the worst passes quickly. Make sure to remind yourself of this fact while you are in the throes of an attack.

One or Two Attacks Doesn't Make a Disorder. Having a panic attack periodically doesn't mean you are crazy, broken, or destined for a life of unexpected panic. Remember that up to one third of people have a panic attack at some point in their life but less than 3% develop panic disorder. Remind yourself of these facts.

Be Aware of Your Panic Triggers. Different people, places, or things set off panic attacks in different people. Develop an aware-ness of your panic triggers. Do attacks tend to happen in the morn-ing, at night, or while sleeping? Do they happen only around certain people or places? Are you having attacks after consuming caffeine, on days when you had little sleep the night before, or after your stress level reaches a certain point? Be a good detective and identify the triggers that lead to your distress.

TREATMENT WORKS. The good news is that there are effective treatments for panic when it begins to cause significant disruption in your daily life. In addition to a variety of self-help techniques, including the ones mentioned here and elsewhere,[3] various talk therapies and medications are available (see Chapter 10 for a discussion of different psychotherapies and medications for anxiety). In other words, you do not have to spend the rest of your life trying to prevent the next panic attack.

Breathing

Yes, I'm recommending breathing exercises once again. Why? Because they work. In addition to the breathing scripts provided in earlier chapters, what follows is one that works well for preventing and getting through a panic attack.

> **Breathing exercises work.**

Although not technically diaphragmatic breathing, one-nostril breathing is an effective way to relax and calm your mind and body. One-nostril breathing is practiced regularly in yoga. It is believed that breathing through your left nostril produces a sense of soothing and calmness whereas breathing through your right nose increases energy. Although I can't confirm or dispute the reported benefits of left-nostril breathing versus right-nostril breathing, my guess is that focusing on one side forces you to slow down your breathing and focus on the present, both which are helpful for reducing anxiety. Here is a sample script you can use.[4]

---

[3]http://www.anxietybc.com/sites/default/files/adult_hmpanic.pdf
[4]From *Relaxation and Wellness Techniques: Mastering the Mind–Body Connection* [CD], by M. Karapetian Alvord, B. Zucker, and B. Alvord. Copyright 2013 by Research Press. Adapted with permission.

First, breathe out completely—blow out as much air as possible, like you are deflating a balloon—until you have let out all the air. Now, take your finger and close one nostril—press in against your nose and hold it. Hold that nostril closed while you close your mouth. Now, slowly breathe in and out through the one open nostril. Keep holding the other nostril closed and keep your mouth closed as well the whole time. Now do it again, slowly breathe in through one nostril, for the count of 5—1, 2, 3, 4, 5, and out—1, 2, 3, 4, 5. Again, in 1, 2, 3, 4, 5, and out 1, 2, 3, 4, 5. Keep going, increasing to 6: breathe in 1, 2, 3, 4, 5, 6, and out 1, 2, 3, 4, 5, 6. Make sure to pace your out breath so it is slow enough to cover the length of the counting. Continue the process until you reach 10.

When breathing this way, you can use the same nostril or switch between nostrils—breathing in through one and out through the other, or breathing in and out through one then switching and breathing in and out through the other. Any combination is fine, the key is to keep only one nostril open at a time while closing your mouth.

Listen to Your Inner Voice

Not to be confused with your inner child, your inner voice is filled with sage advice and guidance. Rely on it as often as you can. In *The Complete Anxiety Treatment and Homework Planner,*[5] psychologist and author Art Jongsma provides rules that can help people deal with panic. The first is to remember that feelings of anxiety and panic

---

[5]From *The Complete Anxiety Treatment and Homework Planner* (p. 176), by A. E. Jongsma, 2004, New York, NY: Wiley. Copyright 2004 by Wiley. Adapted with permission.

are nothing more than an exaggeration of normal bodily reactions to stress. They are no more extreme or intense than what other people experience—those with panic just think they are. Also, these bodily sensations are not harmful or dangerous, just unpleasant. Remember that nothing bad will happen to you simply because of a panic attack. So it's also important to stop adding to panic with frightening thoughts about what is happening and where it might lead. This is what's called *awfulizing*, which is a lot like catastrophizing in the sense that you blow things out of proportion. Another important rule is to stick with the evidence: Notice only what is really happening in your body when you feel panicky, not what "could," "might," or "will probably" happen. Remind yourself that you should wait and give the fear time to pass without fighting it or running away. Don't label, judge, or avoid it—just accept it. Another tactic is to notice that once you stop adding to fear with frightening thoughts, it starts to fade away—you stop being your own worst enemy. As I mentioned above, panic lasts only a few minutes. Don't give it any added help with your unhelpful thoughts. Jongsma reminds his readers to think about the progress they have made, despite all of the difficulties, and how pleased they will be when they succeed this time. There is no better feeling than one of victory over panic. Last, when you begin to feel better, look around and start to plan what to do next. And when you are ready to go on, start off in an easy, relaxed way—without effort or hurrying.

Stop Catastrophizing

As discussed in Chapter 1, people who engage in catastrophic thinking believe that the worst will happen, no matter what the circumstances of the situation may be. This type of thinking fuels anxiety, specifically panic. In addition to the decatastrophizing technique described in Chapter 1, the following script[6] can help you put an end to this panic-inducing form of thinking:

> Think about a situation in which you typically jump to the worst-case scenario: It can involve your work, your relationship with your spouse or child, or it can be a social situation. Maybe you are thinking about a request from your boss for a meeting, about an argument with a loved one, a gathering where you said something you regretted, or any other situation. Try to pinpoint thoughts that have made you feel a sense of peril. As you think about this situation, notice how your body feels: Your heart might start racing, you might start breathing faster through your chest, you might feel your face or stomach muscles tighten, or your hands might feel tingly or sweaty. Focus on one circumstance and think about possible catastrophic thoughts.
>
> Then ask yourself, "What catastrophic thoughts are going through my mind?" "What is the worst thing that can happen?" You might have thoughts along the lines of "My boss will fire me," "My partner will leave me," or "I won't have any friends after saying that," or anything else you might think.
>
> Now ask yourself, "How likely is that to happen? Realistically, what are the chances? Can I handle it?" "What facts do I have to support my worst-case scenario? What facts contradict my worst-case scenario? Is there a more realistic scenario?" Take a few moments to think of a more typical, realistic outcome. More realistic thoughts might include, "My boss might give me suggestions or I might even be getting a compliment," "Arguments don't usually lead to someone leaving," and "People won't judge me on just one statement." For the next few moments, let yourself believe in a more realistic thought instead. What would you tell a friend if he or she came to you, freaking out over a worst-case scenario?

---

[6]From *Relaxation and Wellness Techniques: Mastering the Mind–Body Connection* [CD], by M. Karapetian Alvord, B. Zucker, and B. Alvord. Copyright 2013 by Research Press. Adapted with permission.

Notice the changes in your body sensations and feelings that happen as you change your thought—does focusing on a more realistic thought begin to bring down your heart rate and breathing or help your muscles relax? Remember that dwelling on *What if* thoughts often leads to negative conclusions that are blown out of proportion with reality. It can be tricky to challenge these thoughts because they are often habitual and part of your automatic thinking. However, through the practice of challenging these thoughts and focusing on more realistic outcomes, you can bring down your anxiety and learn to calm yourself. Remember, you make choices about what to think, and you have control over your thoughts.

Now, take a deep breath in through your nose and let it travel down to your lower abdomen, hold it, and slowly breathe out through your mouth. Visualize yourself breathing in the more realistic, positive thoughts, and letting go of the most unrealistic thoughts. Notice how changing your thoughts can change your emotions and change your body sensations. In the next weeks, consider recording your catastrophic thoughts and challenging them. The more aware you are of jumping to worst-case scenarios, and the more you practice challenging them, the easier it will become to change the habitual, automatic *What if* thought sequence.

Now gently stretch your fingers, gradually move your head from side to side, and slowly open your eyes.

Stop Overestimating and Underestimating

People who experience panic attacks do a couple of things. First, they overestimate the likelihood that something bad will happen. For example, although fainting in public is possible, it is extremely unlikely. The reality is that the person may feel lightheaded, dizzy, or flushed but will not faint. Second, panic-stricken individuals underestimate their ability to cope when they experience panic. For example, a woman forgets that she has gotten through dozens of panic attacks in her life. Instead of focusing on skills that she has already mastered, such as diaphragmatic breathing and positive self-talk, she tells herself, "This is the one that's going to kill me" or "I can't handle this." Just like with any cognitive distortion, recognizing you are doing it is the first step, and then you have to challenge the accuracy of your thoughts (see Chapter 1 for a refresher on these techniques).

> People who experience panic attacks overestimate the likelihood that something bad will happen.

Interoceptive Exposure: Confront Your Body

Confronting feared bodily symptoms typically associated with panic is a proven method for overcoming panic attacks. Examples of panic-associated symptoms include racing heart, dizziness, and shortness of breath. Through the process of *interoceptive exposure*, you can confront feared bodily sensations head on as you learn that bodily sensations are not dangerous. And if confronted long enough, the anxiety associated with the sensations will decrease or disappear.

Interoceptive exposure begins by engaging in a variety of exercises intended to bring about uncomfortable physical sensations associated with panic. First, you construct a hierarchy of exercises that can produce paniclike symptoms ranging from least to most distressing. Then, you repeatedly expose yourself to the exercises until they no longer cause significant distress. Remember, the goal is to learn that bodily sensations are harmless, whether you are intentionally creating them or experiencing them during a panic attack. Following are seven interoceptive exercises and step-by-step instructions on how to use them. For more information about these exercises and others, see David Barlow and Michelle Craske's book *Mastery of Your Anxiety and Panic: Workbook.*[7] Use the Interoceptive Exercise Hierarchy at http://pubs.apa.org/books/supp/moore to rank the exercises in order of *most fearful* to *least fearful.* Then work your way up the hierarchy.

A WORD OF CAUTION. If possible, you should strongly consider consulting a trained professional if you are interested in engaging in interoceptive exposure. In fact, the Barlow and Craske book referenced previously is best used while working with a therapist. If you are not able or willing to see a mental health professional, I do not recommend you engage in interoceptive exposure alone. Similar to using exposure exercises with phobias, it is important to have a support person available at all times. Self-inducing panic can lead to the same troubling effects one experiences during panic attacks. And using these techniques alone can lead to injury from falling as a result of fainting. In addition to providing physical support, having a friend, loved one, or panic coach available can provide emotional support before, during, and after the exercises, which increases your chances of being successful.

INTEROCEPTIVE EXERCISES. Talk with your doctor before engaging in these exercises if you have a serious medical condition such as heart or lung disease.

1. Take deep and rapid breaths through your mouth for 60 seconds.
2. Spin around in a swivel chair for 60 seconds. You can spin around standing up, but make sure you are near someone who can catch you if you lose your balance.

---

[7]Barlow, D. H., & Craske, M. G. (2006). *Mastery of your anxiety and panic: Workbook.* New York, NY: Oxford University Press.

3. Breathe through a thin straw for 120 seconds.
4. With your eyes closed, shake your head from side to side for 30 seconds.
5. Run or jog in place for 60 seconds.
6. Place a mirror in your lap and stare back into your eyes for 120 seconds.
7. Stare at a spot on the wall for 120 seconds.

PRACTICING INTEROCEPTIVE EXERCISES

1. Before beginning an exercise, remind yourself that bodily sensations can't hurt you. The symptoms you are experiencing are under your control and will go away soon after you stop the exercise. It also may help to remind yourself that you have a support person present who can help calm you down if you become too distressed.
2. Start with the least distressing exercise. Experience the physical sensations as long as you can. Remember, the longer you can stay with the discomfort, the quicker the anxiety will decrease. Fight the urge to stop. Rely on your support person for strength and encouragement.
3. Rest and relax for 2 minutes or until your anxiety level has returned to baseline. Practice the same exercise again. Continue to practice until you can complete the exercise with little or no anxiety. However, it may be unrealistic to expect that your anxiety will completely disappear. The goal is to get it to the point where it is no longer distressing.
4. Work your way up the hierarchy until you have mastered your most distressing physical sensations. There is no expectation regarding when you will reach the top; it varies from person to person. If you work at a comfortable pace, you will eventually get there.

Become More Assertive

A growing body of psychological research shows having a passive communication style contributes to panic attacks in some people. Why? It's believed that passive communicators take on other people's stress while at the same time they are unable to effectively manage their own. What is a passive communication style? In a nutshell, it means not being assertive. This is not to say that a passive style of communication is not a good thing. Passive communicators are seen as friendly, accommodating, and approachable. But, as with most things in life, moderation is the key. Sometimes it's important to be vocal about your wants and needs, and to not let others put their wants and needs before your own. Following are 10 tips for developing your assertiveness.

EVALUATE YOUR STYLE. Before you can change your communication style, it's important to better understand how you interact with others. Are you defensive or do you get upset when someone provides you with constructive criticism? Do you always say yes even when you don't agree? Do you put other people's feelings and needs before yours? The more behaviors you can identify that you want to change, the more successful you'll be in your pursuit of assertiveness.

MAINTAIN A CONFIDENT DEMEANOR. People respect confidence. It doesn't matter if it's real or feigned. Always present yourself as steady, assured, and strong. Make eye contact. Smile when you first meet someone. Dress and groom nicely. Keep your back straight, walk with your head up, and never slouch. Even if you feel weak, defeated, or hopeless, act as if you were in full control.

USE "I" STATEMENTS. "I" statements convey to people that you own your ideas and behavior. "You" statements put people on the defense and make you seem hostile and petty. For example, say "I don't agree with the accusations being made" and not "You are wrong for saying what you said about me."

SHARE YOUR OPINION. It's easy to become overwhelmed and frustrated when talking with opinionated (not necessarily correct) people. Make sure you state your opinion, even if you aren't 100% sure you're correct. Opinions are just opinions. That's why they aren't called facts.

SAY WHAT YOU WANT AND NEED. In general, people aren't good at mind reading. If you want or need something, state what it is. Don't assume that the other person will eventually pick up on your unhappiness or disappointment.

BECOME COMFORTABLE WITH "NO." "Yes" is a lot easier to say than "no"—just ask any parent. Saying "no" doesn't mean that you are unfeeling, uncaring, or unsympathetic. It just means you don't agree with what is being asked of you. If you feel that "no" is just too mean, try adding a "thank you" on the end.

MAKE SURE YOUR MESSAGE IS HEARD AND UNDERSTOOD. Messages of passive communicators often get overlooked or dismissed. If you have a point, state it over and over until it is heard and acknowledged. It's easy for someone to ignore you. It's difficult for someone to counter an opinion when it is heard in its entirety.

KEEP YOUR EMOTIONS UNDER CONTROL. Overly emotional people rarely win conflicts. Plus, they are often dismissed as irrational and unpredictable. If you find yourself getting angry or feeling like crying when confronting someone, excuse yourself, take a few minutes and gain your composure. Once you've done that, you can try again.

SHOW OTHERS EMPATHY. A person who exudes empathy and caring is listened to more closely than someone who seems cold and detached. Gaining someone's attention is half the battle when it comes to getting your needs met. Showing empathy is also a great way to develop new friendships.

DON'T BE IGNORED. Make your presence known to others. Greet people as they walk into the room. Get up from your chair and join the crowd. Speak loudly enough so that the person behind you can hear what you're saying. Don't be afraid to let your light shine.

SUMMARY

A panic attack is one of the most common and distressing symptoms of anxiety. A person experiencing an attack may feel like he or she is choking, having a heart attack, or even dying. The good news is that panic attacks can be managed through a variety of self-help techniques. However, as with all sources of anxiety, consulting a professional may be needed. Here are a few points to take away from this chapter.

- Panic attacks come on quickly and often without warning.
- The worst of a panic attack is typically over within 10 minutes.
- A panic attack won't kill you.
- Panic is a physiological and chemical process.
- Learning to be assertive can help you overcome fear and panic.

CHAPTER 10

WHAT IF I NEED PROFESSIONAL HELP?

There are many ways of getting strong; sometimes talking is the best way.

—Andre Agassi

Even with access to the best self-help books and a strong network of family and friends, it's quite possible that you may need to seek the help of a mental health professional. Whether it is a psychologist or a psychiatrist, a professional counselor, or a clinical social worker, a number of people out there can help you. Although there are a variety of nontraditional methods people use to manage their anxiety (e.g., acupuncture, yoga, massage), the two most common traditional means for treating anxiety are psychotherapy (i.e., talk therapy) and medication.

What type of mental health professional you choose to consult depends on a couple of factors. The first is access. In many areas of the country, clinical social workers and professional counselors outnumber psychologists and psychiatrists. Therefore, based only on sheer numbers, you may decide to go with one of these professionals. Second, your perception about mental health treatment is important. You may want to see a doctor, which means you would seek the help of a psychologist or psychiatrist (see the following table on differences between mental health professionals). You may be against the idea of taking medication. Because prescribing medication is the bread and butter of most psychiatrists, you will want to consult with a psychologist, as most psychologists do not prescribe medication and focus instead on talk therapy. Last, finances may play a role. Psychiatrists tend to be more expensive than psychologists, and psychologists tend to be more expensive than counselors and social workers. However, most mental health professionals take insurance, so if you have insurance, and depending on your coverage, this may be a moot point.

If you find that you are hesitant to consult with any type of mental health professional, you're not alone. Some people associate seeking psychiatric care with weakness. Others may be too embarrassed or ashamed to get help. Some don't trust the profession as a whole. It's understandable. Society tends to label those who need psychological help with pejorative, hurtful, and ignorant terms such as "crazy," "broken," and "nuts." Popular television shows and movies often portray mental health professionals engaged in extremely unethical behavior.

However, consulting a mental health professional is not a sign of weakness. In fact, it's a sign of strength, awareness, and courage. Furthermore, the vast majority of professionals are highly ethical. But if you still find yourself hesitant to contact a mental health professional, you may want to consider seeking the counsel of a chaplain, priest, rabbi, imam, or other religious/spiritual advisor. Many have training in professional counseling, and most have a depth of wisdom, knowledge, and experience that can help you deal with your anxiety.

PSYCHOTHERAPY

Psychotherapy, or what is synonymously referred to as *counseling*, is the process in which a trained professional works with you to address one or multiple psychological issues, which can range from relationship problems to alcohol dependence to severe depression. Through a variety of techniques, the therapist helps you gain awareness of your behaviors, thought patterns, and emotions and how

Types of Mental Health Professionals

Title	Degree	Typical services	Years of education
Psychiatrist	Medical degree with specialization in psychiatry (MD, DO)	Medication management	11–12
Psychologist	Doctoral degree in psychology (PhD, PsyD, EdD)	Psychotherapy and psychological testing	9–11
Social worker	Master's degree in social work (MSW)	Psychotherapy	5–6
Counselor	Master's degree in counseling (MA, MS, MEd)	Psychotherapy	5–6

they affect your day-to-day life. The ultimate goal is to alleviate your emotional discomfort and help you learn new ways of managing life's many challenges.

Forms of Psychotherapy

There are dozens, if not hundreds, of psychotherapies out there. Three of the more prominent ones are psychodynamic, humanistic, and cognitive-behavioral. *Psychodynamic* psychotherapy, often referred to as *insight-oriented therapy*, is based on the principle that internal processes outside of people's conscious awareness influence their behavior and emotions. The goal is to uncover these unconscious processes by exploring how the past is influencing the present. Sigmund Freud is often associated with this type of therapy. *Humanistic* psychotherapy is a holistic approach that stresses the importance

Cognitive-behavioral therapy has the most research supporting its use with anxiety.

of individual, cultural, and social influences on the person's potential and growth as a human being. Like psychodynamic therapy, humanistic therapy is generally nondirective in nature (i.e., the therapist doesn't tell you what to do). The third approach is *cognitive-behavioral* therapy—simply known as CBT. This type of psychotherapy has the most research supporting its use in people with anxiety and is generally considered to be the most effective form of psychotherapy for anxiety disorders. In fact, some mental health professionals consider CBT to be more effective than medication for most, if not all, types of anxiety (panic, posttraumatic stress disorder, phobias, chronic worry).[1]

CBT focuses on a person's thought processes and rigid belief systems. The goals of therapy are (a) to help the person identify dysfunctional thoughts and beliefs, which are often exaggerated and unrealistic; and (b) to replace those dysfunctional thoughts and beliefs with ones that are more realistic, positive, and functional. The CBT therapist works collaboratively with the person. It is quite different from the popular image of psychoanalysis in which the expert sits quietly and listens to the patient say whatever pops into his or her head. In CBT, there are two experts—the patient and the therapist. Together, they closely analyze the long-held beliefs and ideas about people, events, and the world that contribute to the person's anxiety. For example, a person with anxiety may have the dysfunctional thought "I'll never be able to finish my big project at

---

[1]Muse, M. D., Moore, B. A., & Stahl, S. M. (2013). Benefits and challenges of integrated treatment. In S. M. Stahl & B. A. Moore (Eds.), *Anxiety disorders: A guide for integrating psychopharmacology and psychotherapy* (pp. 3–24). New York, NY: Routledge Press.

work. In 10 years at this company, I've never done anything right." The CBT therapist would challenge this thought and highlight the fact that the person feels like he or she has never done anything right but has been kept on as an employee for 10 years. You don't need a PhD to pick up on the distorted thinking here. The problem is that people are good at seeing other people's faulty thinking but terrible at picking up on their own. This is where a therapist comes in handy.

Choosing the Right Therapist

Choosing a good therapist is like choosing a new car. Do your research, shop around, and take a few test drives—meet and talk with several therapists before deciding on one. By doing so, you will increase your chances of making a good choice. Here are a few tips.[2]

MAKE SURE THE PERSON HAS A CURRENT AND VALID STATE LICENSE TO PRACTICE. Each state has its own standards for licensing and certifying mental health professionals. Be aware, as some titles are not regulated. The titles *psychotherapist, therapist,* and *counselor,* for example, are general terms used by some who do not hold a valid license or have not met minimum educational and clinical training standards. The titles *psychologist, psychiatrist, licensed professional counselor, licensed mental health counselor, clinical social worker,* and *licensed marriage and family therapist* are regulated and imply some type of professional license or credential.

FIND A THERAPIST YOU LIKE. Finding the right therapist is crucial to your success in therapy. In fact, research shows that the strength

---

[2]Moore, B. A. (2012, November 8). Kevlar for the mind: Do research, take "test drive" when choosing a therapist. *Military Times.* Retrieved from http://www.navytimes.com/article/20121118/OFFDUTY03/211180329/Kevlar-Mind-Do-research-take-8216-test-drive-when-choosing-therapist

of the therapy relationship, or what's called the *therapeutic alliance*, is the most important ingredient in treatment. Although people define a "good" therapist and therapeutic relationship differently, most believe that certain aspects of both must be present for the process to work. Mutual trust and mutual respect must be present. You should feel that your therapist understands your situation and is supportive of your needs. And although it can take time, you must be able to be open and honest with your therapist. Does this mean that if you don't like your therapist or therapy, then you should quit? Not necessarily. Therapy is meant to be difficult. At times your therapist will likely say or do things that may challenge you and stretch your limits. You won't always agree with what he or she says. But if you find yourself dreading your appointments because you feel your therapist is disinterested or judgmental, you should find a new one.

ASK A FRIEND OR FAMILY MEMBER. The best source of unbiased information about most things comes from family and friends. Chances are there is someone in your life who has seen a mental health professional. Ask them about their experiences and for recommendations. But don't rely solely on family or friends; you can also find information on and recommendations for mental health professionals on websites like *Angie's List* (http://www.angieslist. com/). For more information on choosing the right therapist, visit the American Psychological Association website (http://www.apa. org/helpcenter/choose-therapist.aspx).

MEDICATION

Medication can be an effective approach for managing anxiety. However, contrary to popular belief, medication will not cure your anxiety. And as I said above, research indicates that it's not quite as effective as psychotherapy for anxiety disorders. However, medication is helpful in many cases. Below are some of the more commonly used medications for anxiety.

> **Medication will not cure your anxiety.**

Antidepressants

The most commonly used medications to treat anxiety are antidepressants called *selective serotonin reuptake inhibitors*, or SSRIs for short. SSRIs manipulate the chemical in the brain called *serotonin*, which is believed to be linked to anxiety. It may seem odd that a person with anxiety would be prescribed an antidepressant. It's really not. Serotonin is related to both depression and anxiety, as well as playing a role in sleep, appetite, sexual functioning, and myriad other things. These medications are known as *antidepressants* because they were first identified to combat depressive symptoms before they were known to also be effective in treating anxiety.

The more common SSRIs include fluoxetine (Prozac), sertraline (Zoloft), paroxetine (Paxil), citalopram (Celexa), and escitalopram (Lexapro). SSRIs are considered to be relatively safe medications, but they do carry the risk of troubling side effects. The most commonly reported side effects include sexual dysfunction in both men and women and stomach discomfort. Specifically, the sexual side effects include disruption in both desire and performance, and the stomach discomfort includes cramping, diarrhea, and nausea. These side effects cause some people to stop taking the medication. Another problem is that it can take time for SSRIs to work; some individuals may not see significant benefits for 4 to 6 weeks. Consequently, many people stop taking the medication before sufficient time to see effects has elapsed, because they believe it is not working.

Benzodiazepines

Benzodiazepines are a class of drugs that are frequently used for the short-term management of anxiety. The most commonly prescribed benzodiazepines are alprazolam (Xanax), clonazepam (Klonopin), diazepam (Valium), lorazepam (Ativan), and temazepam (Restoril, generally reserved for anxiety-related sleep problems). Like alcohol, these medications are great at inducing relaxation, reducing muscle tension, and providing an overall feeling of calmness. The effects are felt almost immediately. However, the safety risks with benzodiazepines are greater than with the SSRIs. These medications do not mix well with alcohol, prescription narcotics (codeine, hydrocodone, methadone), or some sleep medications (Ambien, Lunesta). They are also not recommended for use in people with obstructive sleep apnea or a history of alcohol or drug abuse.

The most common side effects of benzodiazepines include drowsiness, dizziness, forgetfulness, slurred speech, and even depression. And although they are a small minority, some people develop a psychological and physical dependence on these drugs. If benzodiazepines are used for a long period of time, it can be very difficult to wean off of them. Patients who decide to stop taking the medication must do so under the supervision of a health care provider. Stopping the medication too quickly, particularly at higher doses, can potentially lead to seizures, although this is quite rare.

Buspirone

Buspirone (Buspar) is another medication that manipulates serotonin. As with SSRIs, it can take weeks before the person notices any improvement with buspirone. The main benefit of buspirone is that there are no abuse or dependency issues as there are with the benzodiazepines. It can be taken for long periods of time, and it is relatively easy to wean off of once it is no longer needed. It also does not appear to induce the same level of sexual dysfunction as do the SSRIs. The most common side effect is a feeling of lightheadedness shortly after taking buspirone. Less common side effects include headaches, nausea, insomnia, and restlessness.

Other Medications

Mental health professionals use a variety of other medications to treat anxiety, but they are not called "anxiety medications." *Serotonin-norepinephrine reuptake inhibitors*, or SNRIs, are an example. Similar to the SSRIs, SNRIs increase the level of serotonin in the brain. However, they also increase the neurotransmitter norepinephrine, which also plays a role in anxiety. Common examples of SNRIs are venlafaxine (Effexor) and duloxetine (Cymbalta). Hydroxyzine, a generic antihistamine like Benadryl, is occasionally used for the short-term treatment of anxiety. Its most troubling side effect is sleepiness, which limits its use in many people. Another class of medications that have gained popularity in treating anxiety is atypical antipsychotics; quetiapine (Seroquel) and risperidone (Risperdal) are examples. Like the *antidepressant* label, the *antipsychotic* label is confusing when it comes to treating anxiety. But like antidepressants, antipsychotic medications influence a number of chemicals in the brain and are effective for more than just the symptoms associated with the name. The side effects of these medications are significant, however, and may outweigh their benefits. The side effects include weight gain, increased risk of diabetes, and increased cholesterol levels.

A Word of Caution

The decision by pregnant women to use medication for anxiety is not one that should be made lightly. Benzodiazepines have been shown to lead to birth defects, particularly if taken during the first trimester, although this result is uncommon. Research on the negative impact of SSRIs on the developing fetus is inconclusive at best. However, paroxetine (Paxil) has been designated as a Risk Category D by the U.S. Food and Drug Administration, indicating documented evidence of risk to the human fetus. And although buspirone is generally considered less likely to cause harm than other anxiety medications, the research in this area is lacking. In addition to possible harm to the fetus, these medications are found in breast milk. They can unintentionally be transferred to the child during feeding, which can potentially lead to such effects in the child as irritability and sedation. If you are pregnant or breast-feeding and taking medication for anxiety, it is important you talk with your primary care physician, obstetrician/gynecologist, or psychiatrist.

PREPARATION FOR THERAPY

Come Prepared With Questions

Seeking the services of a mental health professional is embarrassing for some, as they associate mental health problems with weakness. Others have stereotypes about mental health treatment, fearing, for example, that they will be pressured to take medication or the therapist will only want to talk about their childhood. Gaining clarity at the outset can ease anxiety about the process. That's why—whether you consult with a psychologist, counselor, social worker, or psychiatrist—it's a good idea to come to your first session with a list of questions that you may have about the treatment process. Here is a list of possible questions you might ask.

> Come to your first session with a list of questions.

- What is your theoretical orientation? Why does it work?
- How long will I need to be in treatment?
- What are the benefits and risks of treatment?
- How will I know that I'm better?
- What is my diagnosis?
- How many people have you treated with this condition?
- What caused my current condition?
- What happens if I don't get better?

If your recommended treatment includes medication, be sure to ask these questions:

- Why did you choose this medication over others?
- How does it work?
- What are the side effects?
- What do I do if I have bad side effects?
- How long will the side effects last?
- How long will I need to take the medication?
- Where can I find more information about the medication?
- When should I take the medication? What happens if I miss a dose?
- Does the medication interfere with me driving or working?
- Does the medication interact with any of the other medications I am taking?

Come Prepared With Information

Knowledge is power. In the case of mental health treatment, knowledge helps the mental health professional make an accurate diagnosis and recommend the right treatment. It also ensures that patients have the opportunity to fully express their concerns and adequately describe their anxiety symptoms. Following are several areas to consider before meeting with a therapist. You can write down your answers and refer to them during your first session.

- What anxiety symptoms/problems are of the most concern to me?
- How long have I been having these symptoms/problems?
- Why am I seeking treatment now?
- Does anything help alleviate my anxiety symptoms/problems?
- When, if ever, have I been treated for mental health issues in the past?
- Did a certain type of therapy or medication work best?
- What mental health problems run in my family?
- What medical problems do I have?
- What medications am I taking (name, dose, frequency)?

SUMMARY

Although self-help techniques can be useful, sometimes you may need to consult with a mental health professional. There are a number of effective treatments for anxiety, including talk therapy, medication, or both. Seeking help should be viewed as an opportunity to take care of your emotional health, just like going to see a physician is a way to take care of your physical health. Here are a few points to take away from this chapter.

- Seeking the assistance of a mental health professional should not be viewed as a weakness or a sign that you are "crazy" or "broken."
- It is important to choose a therapist who will be a good fit for you. Shop around. You have options.
- CBT is the most effective talk therapy for anxiety disorders. It is also as effective, if not more so, than medication.
- Come prepared to your first session with a list of questions.

CHAPTER 11

TRY THESE! A YEAR'S WORTH OF QUOTATIONS AND TIPS FOR RELIEVING ANXIETY

Effective techniques for relieving anxiety don't have to be complicated. Often, the most successful techniques are those based more in common sense than in some abstract psychological theory. The following 52 techniques are simple, yet effective. Your goal is to do each one for an entire week. Place a checkmark in the box for the corresponding day after you complete the technique. After 7 days, move on to the next one.

Keep track of those techniques that are most helpful. For those that are not, try to understand why. Although there are no guarantees in life, I'm confident that these simple behaviors will reduce your anxiety. I've also included an anxiety-related quote for each week. Contemplating the messages and meanings of quotes is a great way to learn about you, others, and the world. Ponder one each week and see whether and how it applies to your life. It's quite possible that you'll find a nugget of wisdom that will help you manage your anxiety.

✎ Week 1: Take a warm bath or shower before bed.

Warm water relaxes your muscles, dilates your blood vessels, and increases oxygen flow to your body. If for some reason you are not able to take a nightly shower or soak, curl up under a heating blanket turned on low for 10 to 15 minutes, and you can get a similar effect.

M	T	W	T	F	S	S

On a scale of 1 to 10, how helpful was this simple exercise in reducing your anxiety? _____ Will you use this technique in the future? _____ If not, why? _____

Quote: Suspense is worse than disappointment.

—Robert Burns

✎ Week 2: Light a scented candle.

Aromatherapy has been used to relieve anxiety and stress for centuries. You can even combine this week with Week 1.

M	T	W	T	F	S	S

On a scale of 1 to 10, how helpful was this simple exercise in reducing your anxiety? _____ Will you use this technique in the future? _____ If not, why? _____

Quote: Anxiety is love's greatest killer. It makes others feel as you might when a drowning man holds on to you. You want to save him, but you know he will strangle you with his panic.

—Anais Nin

🖉 Week 3: Draw, color, or paint a picture.

Art allows you to express your creativity while distracting you from the hassles of everyday life. Spend a few minutes each day letting your creative juices flow.

M	T	W	T	F	S	S

On a scale of 1 to 10, how helpful was this simple exercise in reducing your anxiety? _____ Will you use this technique in the future? _____ If not, why? _____

Quote: A crust eaten in peace is better than a banquet partaken in anxiety.

—Aesop

🖉 Week 4: Listen to your favorite music.

Research shows that listening to music decreases arousal and promotes relaxation. But be careful not to turn it up too loud. Excessive noise can lead to increased stress.

M	T	W	T	F	S	S

On a scale of 1 to 10, how helpful was this simple exercise in reducing your anxiety? _____ Will you use this technique in the future? _____ If not, why? _____

Quote: The components of anxiety, stress, fear, and anger do not exist independently of you in the world. They simply do not exist in the physical world, even though we talk about them as if they do.

—Wayne Dyer

🖉 Week 5: Sit quietly and see how many pleasant childhood memories you can recall.

Conjuring up positive childhood memories stimulates positive thoughts and feelings. If you experienced a difficult childhood and are unable to recall any pleasant memories, rely on some from your adult life.

M	T	W	T	F	S	S

On a scale of 1 to 10, how helpful was this simple exercise in reducing your anxiety? _____ Will you use this technique in the future? _____ If not, why? _____

Quote: Anxiety is the dizziness of freedom.

—Soren Kierkegaard

🖉 Week 6: Do something that you've been putting off.

Procrastination causes you to feel overwhelmed. Even doing small things you've been putting off can make your life seem less chaotic. This could be as simple as paying a bill, reorganizing a pantry shelf, or dropping off some used clothes at the local donation site.

M	T	W	T	F	S	S

On a scale of 1 to 10, how helpful was this simple exercise in reducing your anxiety? _____ Will you use this technique in the future? _____ If not, why? _____

Quote: Nothing in the affairs of men is worthy of great anxiety.

—Plato

🖉 Week 7: Learn a new joke.

Laughing has many healing properties. If you're not any good at coming up with jokes, try www.ajokeaday.com, which will deliver a new, clean joke to your inbox each day.

M	T	W	T	F	S	S

On a scale of 1 to 10, how helpful was this simple exercise in reducing your anxiety? _____ Will you use this technique in the future? _____ If not, why? _____

Quote: Anxiety does not empty tomorrow of its sorrows, but only empties today of its strength.

—Charles Spurgeon

🖉 Week 8: Tell someone a joke.

Don't let your new jokes go to waste. Making other people laugh promotes a sense of connectedness and self-worth.

M	T	W	T	F	S	S

On a scale of 1 to 10, how helpful was this simple exercise in reducing your anxiety? _____ Will you use this technique in the future? _____ If not, why? _____

Quote: In almost everything that touches our everyday life on earth, God is pleased when we're pleased. He wills that we be as free as birds to soar and sing our maker's praise without anxiety.

—Aiden Wilson Tozer

🖋 Week 9: Take off your shoes.

The more stylish shoes become, the more uncomfortable they seem to be. When possible, take off your shoes at work and home. It will help you relax.

M	T	W	T	F	S	S

On a scale of 1 to 10, how helpful was this simple exercise in reducing your anxiety? _____ Will you use this technique in the future? _____
If not, why? _____

Quote: There is no such thing as pure pleasure; some anxiety always goes with it.

—Ovid

🖋 Week 10: Reach out to a family member or friend over the phone, text, or social media site.

Developing and maintaining a strong social support system is a great buffer against stress. Spending a few minutes each day catching up with those you care about but don't see often can pay huge dividends.

M	T	W	T	F	S	S

On a scale of 1 to 10, how helpful was this simple exercise in reducing your anxiety? _____ Will you use this technique in the future? _____
If not, why? _____

Quote: There is great beauty in going through life without anxiety or fear. Half our fears are baseless, and the other half discreditable.

—Christian Nestell Bovee

🖉 Week 11: Go for a short drive.

Taking a drive can be relaxing. It gives you a chance to collect your thoughts after a hard day. It doesn't have to be long—just a few trips around the neighborhood or to the store and back is all that's needed. But stay away from the freeway and other heavy traffic areas. Getting stuck in traffic will get you even more stressed.

M	T	W	T	F	S	S

On a scale of 1 to 10, how helpful was this simple exercise in reducing your anxiety? _____ Will you use this technique in the future? _____ If not, why? _____

Quote: Neither comprehension nor learning can take place in an atmosphere of anxiety.

—Rose Kennedy

🖉 Week 12: Turn off the television if no one is watching it.

Life is filled with background noise, which contributes to anxiety. A little less is a good thing. Plus, it saves energy and money.

M	T	W	T	F	S	S

On a scale of 1 to 10, how helpful was this simple exercise in reducing your anxiety? _____ Will you use this technique in the future? _____ If not, why? _____

Quote: Anything you're trying to will is focused on the future; it's always associated with some sort of anxiety that makes the present moment somewhat uncomfortable.

—Martha Beck

✎ Week 13: Write down as many positive things about yourself or your life that you can think of.

Positive affirmation is a great way to increase self-esteem and counter negative thoughts.

M	T	W	T	F	S	S

On a scale of 1 to 10, how helpful was this simple exercise in reducing your anxiety? _____ Will you use this technique in the future? _____ If not, why? _____

Quote: I always say I am a realist, and my mom says, "No, you just have anxiety."

—Jessica Chastain

✎ Week 14: Avoid someone or something that makes you anxious.

Generally, avoidance is not a healthy strategy for dealing with anxiety. But, in some instances, staying away from people, places, or things that make you anxious can be helpful.

M	T	W	T	F	S	S

On a scale of 1 to 10, how helpful was this simple exercise in reducing your anxiety? _____ Will you use this technique in the future? _____ If not, why? _____

Quote: A mistake in judgment isn't fatal, but too much anxiety about judgment is.

—Pauline Kael

🖉 Week 15: Write a poem.

Writing, particularly creative writing, keeps the mind focused and anxious thoughts at bay.

M	T	W	T	F	S	S

On a scale of 1 to 10, how helpful was this simple exercise in reducing your anxiety? _____ Will you use this technique in the future? _____ If not, why? _____

Quote: The natural role of twentieth-century man is anxiety.

—Norman Mailer

🖉 Week 16: Sort through and organize old pictures.

Similar to writing a poem, this activity keeps the mind focused. It also creates a sense of nostalgia, which can be very comforting. If you are short on time, just spend a few minutes just looking at them.

M	T	W	T	F	S	S

On a scale of 1 to 10, how helpful was this simple exercise in reducing your anxiety? _____ Will you use this technique in the future? _____ If not, why? _____

Quote: What else does anxiety about the future bring you but sorrow upon sorrow?

—Thomas Kempis

✏ Week 17: Play a video/computer game.

Yes, your kids may know something you don't. Video/computer games can be a good distraction from the daily hassles of life—but only in moderation, and nothing violent before bed!

M	T	W	T	F	S	S

On a scale of 1 to 10, how helpful was this simple exercise in reducing your anxiety? _____ Will you use this technique in the future? _____ If not, why? _____

Quote: Freedom from care and anxiety of mind is a blessing, which I apprehend such people enjoy in higher perfection than most others, and is of the utmost consequence.

—William Falconer

✏ Week 18: Indulge yourself.

Sometimes it's okay to give in to your desires. Have a second piece of chocolate, add the cheese to the hamburger, or sleep until noon on the weekend. If your health allows it, give in to your desires. Once in a while won't hurt you.

M	T	W	T	F	S	S

On a scale of 1 to 10, how helpful was this simple exercise in reducing your anxiety? _____ Will you use this technique in the future? _____ If not, why? _____

Quote: To hear the phrase "our only hope" always makes one anxious, because it means that if the only hope doesn't work, there is nothing left.

—Lemony Snicket

Week 19: Give in on something.

People with anxiety have high standards for just about everything. Relax your standards on at least one thing each day. An example may be letting your kid's room go a day without being cleaned.

M	T	W	T	F	S	S

On a scale of 1 to 10, how helpful was this simple exercise in reducing your anxiety? _____ Will you use this technique in the future? _____ If not, why? _____

Quote: Worrying is carrying tomorrow's load with today's strength—carrying two days at once. It is moving into tomorrow ahead of time. Worrying doesn't empty tomorrow of its sorrow, it empties today of its strength.

—Corrie ten Boom

Week 20: Stay in the present during conversations.

A hazard of multitasking is that you probably aren't giving your full attention during conversations with your loved ones. When talking with your spouse, friends, children, or other loved ones, devote 100% of your attention to what's being said. Make them feel like what they are talking about is the only thing that matters.

M	T	W	T	F	S	S

On a scale of 1 to 10, how helpful was this simple exercise in reducing your anxiety? _____ Will you use this technique in the future? _____ If not, why? _____

Quote: The more you pray, the less you'll panic. The more you worship, the less you worry. You'll feel more patient and less pressured.

—Rick Warren

✎ Week 21: Visualize a successful outcome.

Research shows that visualizing successful outcomes increases performance. Reduce your anxiety, stress, and worry by seeing yourself overcome at least one future obstacle each day. You may want to review the imagery exercises in Chapter 6.

M	T	W	T	F	S	S

On a scale of 1 to 10, how helpful was this simple exercise in reducing your anxiety? _____ Will you use this technique in the future? _____ If not, why? _____

Quote: Anxiety's like a rocking chair. It gives you something to do, but it doesn't get you very far.

—Jodi Picoult

✎ Week 22: Sing while you wait.

Waiting is a source of stress for most anyone. Singing while you are standing in line at the store, stuck in traffic, or sitting in the doctor's waiting room is a great way to reduce your stress and divert your attention away from anxious thoughts. If other people are around, you may want to use your "quiet voice."

M	T	W	T	F	S	S

On a scale of 1 to 10, how helpful was this simple exercise in reducing your anxiety? _____ Will you use this technique in the future? _____ If not, why? _____

Quote: To venture causes anxiety, but not to venture is to lose one's self . . . And to venture in the highest is precisely to be conscious of one's self.

—Soren Kierkegaard

🖊 Week 23: Turn a need into a like or preference.

There are few things in life that people actually need: Water, food, clothing, and shelter are some of them. Being the best salesman in the tristate area or being liked by everyone is not a need. Identify those likes and preferences you have turned into needs and let go of them.

M	T	W	T	F	S	S

On a scale of 1 to 10, how helpful was this simple exercise in reducing your anxiety? _____ Will you use this technique in the future? _____ If not, why? _____

Quote: Man is not worried by real problems so much as by his imagined anxieties about real problems.

—Epictetus

🖊 Week 24: Hang around nonanxious people.

You've probably heard the phrase "misery loves company." Well, anxiety also loves company. Spend time with someone who you would characterize as not anxious.

M	T	W	T	F	S	S

On a scale of 1 to 10, how helpful was this simple exercise in reducing your anxiety? _____ Will you use this technique in the future? _____ If not, why? _____

Quote: I promise you nothing is as chaotic as it seems. Nothing is worth your health. Nothing is worth poisoning yourself into stress, anxiety, and fear.

—Steve Maraboli

✐ Week 25: Practice yoga.

Yoga is the ancient Hindu practice of using physical poses and postures to bring about emotional, spiritual, and physical balance. (Visit http://www.yoga.com to learn some basic techniques.)

M	T	W	T	F	S	S

On a scale of 1 to 10, how helpful was this simple exercise in reducing your anxiety? _____ Will you use this technique in the future? _____ If not, why? _____

Quote: I've spent most of my life and most of my friendships holding my breath and hoping that when people get close enough they won't leave, and fearing that it's a matter of time before they figure me out and go.

—Shauna Niequist

✐ Week 26: Take a lunch break.

Simple, right? Not for many of us. We are often so busy that we forget to even stop and eat. Make sure you take at least 30 minutes to enjoy your lunch. One trick is to schedule it into your daily routine, like you do everything else.

M	T	W	T	F	S	S

On a scale of 1 to 10, how helpful was this simple exercise in reducing your anxiety? _____ Will you use this technique in the future? _____ If not, why? _____

Quote: Temperamentally anxious people can have a hard time staying motivated, period, because their intense focus on their worries distracts them from their goals.

—Winifred Gallagher

🖉 Week 27: Spend time with a pet.

Pets can be very relaxing and therapeutic. If you don't have a pet, stop by the local animal shelter for 15 minutes and visit with the animals.

M	T	W	T	F	S	S

On a scale of 1 to 10, how helpful was this simple exercise in reducing your anxiety? _____ Will you use this technique in the future? _____
If not, why? _____

Quote: Bodily haste and exertion usually leave our thoughts very much at the mercy of our feelings and imagination.

—George Eliot

🖉 Week 28: Say "hi" and smile when passing a stranger.

When life becomes hectic, we tend to drown out those around us. Being polite and friendly to others will make you feel more connected to those around you, even strangers.

M	T	W	T	F	S	S

On a scale of 1 to 10, how helpful was this simple exercise in reducing your anxiety? _____ Will you use this technique in the future? _____
If not, why? _____

Quote: Though it may feel otherwise, enjoying life is no more dangerous than apprehending it with continuous anxiety and gloom.

—Alain de Botton

Load the mundane and challenging work tasks early in the day. Once they are completed, you can spend the rest of your day doing what you enjoy or what you find interesting. Ending on a positive note is always a good thing.

M	T	W	T	F	S	S

On a scale of 1 to 10, how helpful was this simple exercise in reducing your anxiety? _____ Will you use this technique in the future? _____ If not, why? _____

Quote: One source of frustration in the workplace is the frequent mismatch between what people must do and what people can do. When what they must do exceeds their capabilities, the result is anxiety. When what they must do falls short of their capabilities, the result is boredom. But when the match is just right, the results can be glorious. This is the essence of flow.

—Daniel H. Pink

Find an opportunity to forgive someone for what they did to you. Forgiveness is a great way to let go of anxious and hurtful emotions. Although it's helpful to let the person know you have forgiven them, it's not necessary.

M	T	W	T	F	S	S

On a scale of 1 to 10, how helpful was this simple exercise in reducing your anxiety? _____ Will you use this technique in the future? _____ If not, why? _____

Quote: I like to read and write because it is the ONLY thing that takes my mind off of the real world and my spinning worries. It is a time I can be free of anxiety, worry, and stress. When my life gets hectic I HAVE to read and write or I'll drown.

—Shandy L. Kurth

🖉 Week 31: Write things down.

Your memory might be stronger than the average person's, but it's not perfect. Write down those things that would make you feel anxious or more stressed if you forgot to do them.

M	T	W	T	F	S	S

On a scale of 1 to 10, how helpful was this simple exercise in reducing your anxiety? _____ Will you use this technique in the future? _____ If not, why? _____

Quote: But the Christian also knows that he not only cannot and dare not be anxious, but that there is no need for him to be so. Neither anxiety nor work can secure his daily bread, for bread is the gift of the Father.

—Dietrich Bonhoeffer

🖉 Week 32: Walk slower.

Walking fast creates a sense of urgency when there isn't one. If you find yourself walking fast because you are late, try the next tip.

M	T	W	T	F	S	S

On a scale of 1 to 10, how helpful was this simple exercise in reducing your anxiety? _____ Will you use this technique in the future? _____ If not, why? _____

Quote: Avoiding life, avoiding making any concrete plans for your life—that's just one way you're pretending you can keep bad things from happening to you again.

—Susan Vaught

✎ Week 33: Leave 15 minutes early.

If you are always running behind, it's time to start leaving for work, school, or appointments a little bit earlier.

M	T	W	T	F	S	S

On a scale of 1 to 10, how helpful was this simple exercise in reducing your anxiety? _____ Will you use this technique in the future? _____ If not, why? _____

Quote: It's been my experience that people always assume that generalized anxiety disorder is preferable to social anxiety disorder, because it sounds more vague and unthreatening, but those people are totally wrong. For me, having generalized anxiety disorder is basically like having all of the other anxiety disorders smooshed into one. Even the ones that aren't recognized by modern science. Things like birds-will-probably-smother-me-in-my-sleep anxiety disorder and I-keep-crackers-in-my-pocket-in-case-I-get-trapped-in-an-elevator anxiety disorder. Basically I'm just generally anxious about f***ing everything. In fact, I suspect that's how they came up with the name.

—Jenny Lawson

🖋 Week 34: Let it all out.

Scream, stomp your feet, or punch a pillow. Sometimes you just need to let it all out. Extreme emotional release is not a good strategy as a long-term coping strategy, but it can be in the short term. Just make sure to do it in a place where no one else can hear or see you. If not, things could get awkward.

M	T	W	T	F	S	S

On a scale of 1 to 10, how helpful was this simple exercise in reducing your anxiety? _____ Will you use this technique in the future? _____ If not, why? _____

Quote: Freedom is anxiety's petri dish. If routine blunts anxiety, freedom incubates it. Freedom says, "Even if you don't want to make choices, you have to, and you can never be sure you have chosen correctly." Freedom says, "Even not to choose is to choose." Freedom says, "So long as you are aware of your freedom, you are going to experience the discomfort that freedom brings." Freedom says, "You're on your own. Deal with it."

—Daniel Smith

Week 35: Work in the garden.

Working with flowers can be very relaxing and is a great way to get your mind off things. If you don't have a garden, spend the time creating a simple one.

M	T	W	T	F	S	S

On a scale of 1 to 10, how helpful was this simple exercise in reducing your anxiety? _____ Will you use this technique in the future? _____ If not, why? _____

Quote: Anxiety was born in the very same moment as mankind. And since we will never be able to master it, we will have to learn to live with it—just as we have learned to live with storms.

—Paulo Coelho

Week 36: Pinch yourself.

Each time you have an anxious thought, pinch yourself. Not only does it distract your mind, it associates anxious thinking with something uncomfortable. After time, you will train your mind and body to avoid anxious thoughts because they have become associated with physical discomfort.

M	T	W	T	F	S	S

On a scale of 1 to 10, how helpful was this simple exercise in reducing your anxiety? _____ Will you use this technique in the future? _____ If not, why? _____

Quote: We are tempted to believe that certain achievements and possessions will give us enduring satisfaction. We are invited to imagine ourselves scaling the steep cliff face of happiness in order to reach a wide, high plateau on which we will live out the rest of our lives; we are not reminded that soon after gaining the summit, we will be called down again into fresh lowlands of anxiety and desire.

—Alain de Botton

Week 37: Drink 8 cups of water a day.

The recommended daily intake of water is 8 cups. If you are like most people, you probably only drink half that amount. Inadequate water intake can lead to dehydration, which leads to fatigue, inefficiency, and increased stress.

M	T	W	T	F	S	S

On a scale of 1 to 10, how helpful was this simple exercise in reducing your anxiety? _____ Will you use this technique in the future? _____ If not, why? _____

Quote: Let pressure pass over and through you. That way you can't be harmed by it.

—Brian Herbert

Week 38: Put a positive spin on things.

When something happens that makes you anxious, look for ways to put a positive spin on it. For example, if your boss tells you to have a presentation ready by the end of the day, instead of becoming fearful or worried, tell yourself, "It's great that my boss thinks so highly of my abilities that he gave me this last minute project."

M	T	W	T	F	S	S

On a scale of 1 to 10, how helpful was this simple exercise in reducing your anxiety? _____ Will you use this technique in the future? _____ If not, why? _____

Quote: In bed our yesterdays are too oppressive: If a man can only get up, though it be but to whistle or to smoke, he has a present which offers some resistance to the past—sensations which assert themselves against tyrannous memories.

—George Eliot

Week 39: Drink herbal tea.

Herbal tea has been shown to be calming and relaxing. But make sure it is decaffeinated. As discussed in Chapter 4, caffeine can lead to panic.

M	T	W	T	F	S	S

On a scale of 1 to 10, how helpful was this simple exercise in reducing your anxiety? _____ Will you use this technique in the future? _____ If not, why? _____

Quote: Her little butterfly soul fluttered incessantly between memory and dubious expectation.

—George Eliot

Week 40: The "grand scheme."

Each time you find yourself worrying or obsessing about a problem or concern, ask yourself, "In the grand scheme of things, does this really matter?" In most cases you will find that it doesn't.

M	T	W	T	F	S	S

On a scale of 1 to 10, how helpful was this simple exercise in reducing your anxiety? _____ Will you use this technique in the future? _____ If not, why? _____

Quote: All the greatest blessings are a source of anxiety, and at no time should fortune be less trusted than when it is best; to maintain prosperity there is need of other prosperity, and in behalf of the prayers that have turned out well we must make still other prayers. For everything that comes to us from chance is unstable, and the higher it rises, the more liable it is to fall. Moreover, what is doomed to perish brings pleasure to no one; very wretched, therefore, and not merely short, must the life of those be who work hard to gain what they must work harder to keep. By great toil they attain what they wish, and with anxiety hold what they have attained; meanwhile they take no account of time that will never more return.

—Lucius Annaeus Seneca

🖉 Week 41: Get some sun.

Moderate exposure to sunlight can improve your mood and physical health. Spend a few minutes letting the sun bathe over you.

M	T	W	T	F	S	S

On a scale of 1 to 10, how helpful was this simple exercise in reducing your anxiety? _____ Will you use this technique in the future? _____ If not, why? _____

Quote: We are faced with choices every moment of our lives. Whatever choice we exercise must make us comfortable and at peace. Choices that are made out of fear and anxiety often do not lead to right action.

—Sasha Samy

🖉 Week 42: Ask someone for help.

You don't have to do everything by yourself. Ask those around you to pitch in. Relieving your burden by just a small amount can help with your anxiety.

M	T	W	T	F	S	S

On a scale of 1 to 10, how helpful was this simple exercise in reducing your anxiety? _____ Will you use this technique in the future? _____ If not, why? _____

Quote: I have always felt that fear possesses such great power, enough to paralyze and quake an individual. Pondering this, I realized that the source of fear's power comes from within me. So, I ask myself, does that not make me the powerful one?

—Richelle E. Goodrich

✎ Week 43: Play with a childhood toy.

The nostalgia associated with childhood toys can be very therapeutic. If you don't have one already, you can find one on eBay.

M	T	W	T	F	S	S

On a scale of 1 to 10, how helpful was this simple exercise in reducing your anxiety? _____ Will you use this technique in the future? _____ If not, why? _____

Quote: My mind turned by anxiety, or other cause, from its scrutiny of blank paper, is like a lost child—wandering the house, sitting on the bottom step to cry.

—Virginia Woolf

✎ Week 44: Don't check work e-mail at home.

Leave the work e-mail at the office. It will be waiting on you in the morning.

M	T	W	T	F	S	S

On a scale of 1 to 10, how helpful was this simple exercise in reducing your anxiety? _____ Will you use this technique in the future? _____ If not, why? _____

Quote: It ain't no use putting up your umbrella till it rains!

—Alice Caldwell Rice

🖉 Week 45: Rock . . . the chair, not the music.

The back-and-forth motion of rocking can be very relaxing.

M	T	W	T	F	S	S

On a scale of 1 to 10, how helpful was this simple exercise in reducing your anxiety? _____ Will you use this technique in the future? _____
If not, why? _____

Quote: Behind every flinch is a fear or an anxiety—sometimes rational, sometimes not. Without the fear, there is no flinch. But wiping out the fear isn't what's important—facing it is.

—Julien Smith

🖉 Week 46: Play a card game.

Few things are better at taking your mind off of your worries than playing a game of solitaire or free cell.

M	T	W	T	F	S	S

On a scale of 1 to 10, how helpful was this simple exercise in reducing your anxiety? _____ Will you use this technique in the future? _____
If not, why? _____

Quote: While fear depletes power, faith gives wings for the soul's elevation.

—T. F. Hodge

🖋 Week 47: Stretch.

Get up and stretch for a few minutes at least once every couple of hours. Stretching relieves muscle tension and reduces back pain.

M	T	W	T	F	S	S

On a scale of 1 to 10, how helpful was this simple exercise in reducing your anxiety? _____ Will you use this technique in the future? _____ If not, why? _____

Quote: When I don't have something to worry about, I worry. Nothing comes so naturally to a human being as anxiety and worry.

—Brian Richardson

🖋 Week 48: Use a heating pad.

Life produces sore and tight muscles. A heating pad is a great way to relieve muscle strain and promote a sense of relaxation.

M	T	W	T	F	S	S

On a scale of 1 to 10, how helpful was this simple exercise in reducing your anxiety? _____ Will you use this technique in the future? _____ If not, why? _____

Quote: We live in the hope that life will be different. Just a little more substance perhaps in the intrinsic frailty of the days. Such resignation frightens me. Between gunshots I get drunk. In secret, all knowledge becomes anxiety.

—Floriano Martins

✏ Week 49: Get a massage.

It's unlikely that you can get a full massage every day, but asking someone for a 5-minute shoulder or neck rub can do wonders. It's generally best to ask someone you already know!

M	T	W	T	F	S	S

On a scale of 1 to 10, how helpful was this simple exercise in reducing your anxiety? _____ Will you use this technique in the future? _____ If not, why? _____

Quote: What some call health, if purchased by perpetual anxiety about diet, isn't much better than tedious disease.

—George Dennison Prentice

✏ Week 50: Let someone else drive.

Driving causes us to be focused on everything but ourselves. Let someone else drive, and focus your mind on pleasant and relaxing thoughts. If this isn't possible, turn off the radio and cell phone and focus exclusively on driving.

M	T	W	T	F	S	S

On a scale of 1 to 10, how helpful was this simple exercise in reducing your anxiety? _____ Will you use this technique in the future? _____ If not, why? _____

Quote: All this wondering was the weather vane on top of the building of unrest and of discontent.

—John Steinbeck

✎ Week 51: Avoid processed food.

Processed foods strain your digestive system. Switch to whole-grain, high-fiber, and nongreasy foods for a week and see how you feel.

M	T	W	T	F	S	S

On a scale of 1 to 10, how helpful was this simple exercise in reducing your anxiety? _____ Will you use this technique in the future? _____
If not, why? _____

Quote: We live only a few conscious decades, and we fret ourselves enough for several lifetimes.

—Christopher Hitchens

✎ Week 52: Do something nice for someone.

Research shows that doing something nice for someone else, no matter how small it may seem, can improve your mood.

M	T	W	T	F	S	S

On a scale of 1 to 10, how helpful was this simple exercise in reducing your anxiety? _____ Will you use this technique in the future? _____
If not, why? _____

Quote: In any weather, at any hour of the day or night, I have been anxious to improve the nick of time, and notch it on my stick too; to stand on the meeting of two eternities, the past and future, which is precisely the present moment; to toe that line.

—Henry David Thoreau

INDEX

ABOUT THE AUTHOR

Bret A. Moore, PsyD, is licensed as a prescribing psychologist by the New Mexico Board of Psychologist Examiners and is board certified in clinical psychology by the American Board of Professional Psychology. Over the past 15 years he has treated thousands of patients suffering from anxiety with both psychotherapy and medication. He is the author and editor of 13 books, including *Anxiety Disorders: A Guide for Integrating Pharmacotherapy and Psychotherapy, Pharmacotherapy for Psychologists: Prescribing and Collaborative Roles, Handbook of Clinical Psychopharmacology for Psychologists,* and *Treating PTSD in Military Personnel: A Clinical Handbook.* His views on clinical psychology have been quoted in *USA Today, The New York Times,* and *The Boston Globe,* and on CNN and Fox News. He has appeared on NPR, the BBC, and CBC.